CW00539630

ONE DAY
ONE MOMENT

THE RISING CIRCLE

We are an empowering wellness community dedicated to uplifting your vibration and supporting your inward journey. Our wide range of tools, resources and transformative products are thoughtfully curated to enhance your overall well-being.

Like an infinite circle, our spiritual journey has no beginning or end. We continue to expand and evolve, embracing the ever-unfolding possibilities. And just as the sun faithfully rises each day, the radiant light within us also awakens to illuminate our world.

As a compassionate community, we wholeheartedly believe in our collective capacity to rise and shine, co-creating a world brimming with love, understanding, and positive transformation.

Follow us on Instagram and TikTok @TheRisingCircle

Sign up to our weekly newsletter on www.therisingcircle.com

Get in touch via hello@therisingcircle.com

ONE DAY
ONE MOMENT

FOR PEACE AND POSITIVITY

The Rising Circle
Vex King and Kaushal

bluebird
books for life

First published 2024 by Bluebird
an imprint of Pan Macmillan
The Smithson, 6 Briset Street, London EC1M 5NR
EU representative: Macmillan Publishers Ireland Ltd, 1st Floor,
The Liffey Trust Centre, 117–126 Sheriff Street Upper,
Dublin 1, D01 YC43
Associated companies throughout the world
www.panmacmillan.com

ISBN 9781035048564

1 3 5 7 9 8 6 4 2

A CIP catalogue record for this book is available from the British Library.
Design and typesetting by Heather Bowen
Illustrations by Sinead Hayward (pp 43, 281) and Shutterstock
Printed and bound in China

Visit **www.panmacmillan.com/bluebird** to read more about all our books
and to buy them. You will also find features, author interviews and
news of any author events, and you can sign up for e-newsletters
so that you're always first to hear about our new releases.

A MESSAGE JUST FOR YOU

We are proud of you for starting this mindful planning journey, and we understand that finding balance between your professional and personal lives can be a challenge. That is why we have created the *One Day, One Moment* planner – a tool designed to help you achieve your career aspirations without compromising your well-being.

This six-month planner provides a straightforward yet powerful approach to your days. Each day, you will have the opportunity to organize, plan, reflect, review and take steps towards reaching your goals.

We are thrilled to share this creation with you. By taking things one day and one moment at a time, we hope this planner helps you foster ultimate peace and positivity alongside your goals.

With love,
Vex and Kaushal

This planner is dedicated to you.

Embark on this mindful journey one day and one moment at a time. Find that perfect balance of work and self-care on a daily basis.

You deserve to reach your goals without compromising your mind, body and spirit.

You've got this.

My name is . . .

. . . and I am taking one day and one moment
to mindfully plan.

CONTENTS

PLANNING 101

Everything you need to know about planning mindfully

It is time to break down planning in a way that will make your busy, stressful or daunting days more manageable and allow you to tackle them mindfully.

POWER HOUR

A Power Hour is a dedicated and focused hour, at whatever time of the day suits you best, when you take on small, manageable tasks that do not consume a lot of time. It is a chance to efficiently handle quick, often routine activities like emails, placing orders, making short phone calls or tackling small chores on your to-do list.

Getting several small tasks done in one go gives you a feeling of accomplishment and sets a positive tone for the day. It also frees up your mind for more significant and creative work.

Maximize your Power Hour by:

PLANNING AHEAD
Figure out and prioritize small tasks the night before so you can jump right in during your dedicated hour.

LIMITING INTERRUPTIONS
Minimize distractions during this hour to get the most out of your productivity.

SETTING A TIMER
Decide how much time each task gets in order to stay focused and avoid spending too much time on one thing.

CELEBRATING PROGRESS
Give yourself credit for completing each task. It is a positive and motivating way to start your day.

Try these steps, and you will see how a Power Hour can set a productive tone for the rest of your day!

50–10 METHOD

Ever thought about tackling your work in a smarter way? That is where our 50–10 Method comes in. It is a nifty time-management strategy (inspired by the Pomodoro Technique, where you work for 25 minutes, break for 5, and repeat), designed to boost productivity and keep burnout at bay. Here is how it works:

By helping you find the right balance between focused work and smart breaks, our 50–10 Method optimizes productivity, minimizes fatigue and keeps your workflow sustainable. Give it a try and see the difference it can make in managing your tasks!

Focused Work	Break
50 minutes	10 minutes

STEP 1: CHOOSE YOUR TASK
Pick the task you want to focus on, whether it is work-related, a project or studying.

STEP 2: SET A TIMER FOR 50 MINUTES
Use your phone or any timer device to set 50 minutes. During this time, give your full attention to your chosen task.

STEP 3: WORK DILIGENTLY
Dive into your task and stay focused for the entire 50 minutes, avoiding distractions.

STEP 4: TAKE A 10-MINUTE BREAK
When the timer rings, take a dedicated 10-minute break. Step away and do something enjoyable, like meditation, a nature walk or stretching.

STEP 5: REPEAT THE CYCLE
After the break, go back to step one. Choose a new task or stick with the same one. Repeat the 50 minutes of focused work, then take a 10-minute break.

TAKE A LONG BREAK

Make sure you dedicate one hour of your day to a long break away from work. This is important as it will boost your well-being and recharge your energy. Here is what you can do:

EAT WELL AND HYDRATE

Take the time to enjoy a healthy and balanced meal that gives your body the fuel it needs. Stay hydrated by drinking plenty of water. You can mix it up with herbal tea or infused water for some variety.

DIGITAL DETOX

Give your eyes and mind a break from screens by avoiding your phone or other electronic devices during lunch. It is your chance to unplug and relax.

MINDFUL ACTIVITIES

Add some mindfulness to your break with activities like deep breathing, short walks, a bit of yoga, reading, connecting with friends or listening to music or a podcast. These simple activities can help you unwind and make the most of your break.

TIME BLOCKING

Time blocking is a helpful method for becoming more organized and accomplishing tasks throughout the day. It involves allocating specific times for various activities or tasks, whether they are work-related, personal or recreational. This could include work tasks, self-care activities, breaks or a bit of fun – like meeting a friend or getting a haircut. It is a versatile approach that can be applied to any task or activity on your agenda!

When you plan your day ahead of time and schedule specific times for different tasks, you ensure that important activities receive the attention they deserve. This approach is highly effective for managing tasks efficiently and helping you achieve your goals. In essence, time blocking enables you to be more deliberate and proactive with your time. It is like having a roadmap for your work and personal activities, resulting in increased efficiency, reduced stress and improved work–life balance. A helpful tip is to fill out your time-blocking schedule the night before to make the most of the next day.

HOW DO I USE THIS PLANNER?

A simple step-by-step guide on how to use this planner

WEEKDAY PLANNING

Start each day by writing down the date. By doing this, you can monitor tasks completed, trackers, notes, how you felt on that particular day, etc.

MONDAY *6th January 2025*

LIFE WILL TEST ME JUST BEFORE IT WILL BLESS ME

AFFIRMATION
The words we say hold so much power over how we feel. After the date, read the daily affirmation out loud five times for maximum effect!

MINDFUL TRACKER
Use your mindful tracker to ensure you have had enough sleep, audit your mood for the day and monitor your water intake. Sleep is crucial for self-care, healing and productivity. Tracking your mood at the end of the day enhances self-awareness. And a reminder to drink your recommended two litres of water daily will ensure you remain hydrated!

SLEEP TRACKER   MOOD TRACKER   WATER TRACKER

TIME BLOCKING
This is where you can time block your Power Hour, five main tasks of the day from your 50–10 Method, any important meetings, appointments, and even your lunch break. Block your time and schedule accordingly, ultimately using this space to work for you, not against you. The time starts at 5.00 a.m. and ends at 10.00 p.m., so you can include any morning or evening rituals

5.00	
5.30	
6.00	*Walk the dog*
6.30	
7.00	*Breakfast*
7.30	
8.00	*Call doctor*
8.30	*Meet M for coffee*
9.00	
9.30	
10.00	
10.30	
11.00	

you would like to add to keep you accountable or serve as a reminder during the day. We recommend using a pencil or erasable pen so that you can easily switch, swap and edit your day according to your needs.

POWER HOUR

Unload all of the little things you need to tick off during your Power Hour. Scribble down anything that comes to mind. This should only take you a few minutes. Then, spend the next Power Hour completing and ticking off each task. This is a great way to beat procrastination and stay focused throughout your day.

POWER HOUR

- ○ *Book train tickets*
- ○ *Send over photos*
- ○ *Email D about lunch*
- ○ *Sort out expenses*
- ○ *Text bestie back*
- ○ *Organize work desk*

50-10 METHOD

Write down your five most important tasks that need working on or completing that day. You can repeat tasks if you wish, but make sure you take that 10-minute break at the end of every 50 minutes to keep yourself focused and balanced during your work hours.

50-10 METHOD

1. *Research party venue* ○
2. *1:1 meeting with G* ○
3. *Call K to plan project* ○
4. *Complete application* ○
5. *Read through draft* ○

NOTES

Use this area to make any notes for the day. Whether they are reminders, notes from video calls, or anything else, jot them down here. If you are feeling stressed during the day, there is a QR code at the bottom that you can scan, which will take you directly to our 10-minute guided meditations. Feel free to use this as much as you like during your 10-minute breaks.

MINI MINDFUL MOMENT

Think of these three questions as your moment in the day to take some time out to reflect. You will encounter something positive to remember each day, a unique gratitude prompt and a self-care reminder. This can be a beautiful way to implement our 1–1–1 Method, as seen in *The Greatest Manifestation Book*. With this method, you create three non-negotiables that you must do for yourself and your well-being – one daily, one weekly and one monthly.

One moment I want to remember from today is . . .

My morning chat with C

What am I grateful for?

My lunchtime walk in the sun

I have looked after myself today by . . .

Taking the time to meditate before work

WEEKEND PLANNING

It is essential to have balance in your week, but we understand that you may need some space for lists, goal planning and making notes, etc.

WEEKEND AFFIRMATION

Affirmations will serve as an anchor for your everyday routine, including weekends. Do not forget to recite the daily affirmation out loud five times during your weekend for maximum effect!

SATURDAY AND SUNDAY *11th & 12th January 2025*

I COUNT MY BLESSINGS, TODAY AND EVERY DAY

TO-DO LISTS

You will have an area to write down any important to-dos. This is a perfect way to stay on top of anything you need to do during the weekends.

SATURDAY LIST

1. Renew insurance ○
2. Prep Sunday lunch ○
3. Pick up flowers for H ○
4. Dinner with T ○
5. Hair @ 10am ○

SUNDAY LIST

1. Pick up fruit and veg ○
2. Wash the car ○
3. Iron clothes ○
4. Walk with P ○
5. Fix the kitchen cabinet ○

WEEKEND REMINDERS

To ensure that you are looking after yourself during the weekends, there is a little tick-box section to remind you to complete a digital detox (we recommend at least one hour over the weekend, but the longer, the better!), to do something self-care-related on Sunday, and to have some good old-fashioned fun during your weekend too. Self-care activities could be as simple as sitting in the garden while you mindfully drink a cup of coffee or calling a friend for a catch-up. You do not need to do all three things on one day, but use these as a reminder to do them at some point over the weekend.

DIGITAL DETOX ✓   SELF-CARE SUNDAY ✓   HAVE FUN ✓

GOALS FOR THE NEXT WEEK

If you would like to plan ahead and jot down any goals for the coming week, use this space to list them so that you do not forget them. Make sure to review and incorporate them into your Power Hour or time blocking for the next week.

MIND DUMP

To clear your mind of anything else, there is some space to write, doodle or even journal any thoughts that you may be holding on to. This is a great way to end the week and start fresh on Monday.

MINDFUL ACTIVITY

Every weekend, you will encounter a mindful activity to engage in. These activities are designed to help you relax, find peace and slow down, which all contribute to long-term productivity.

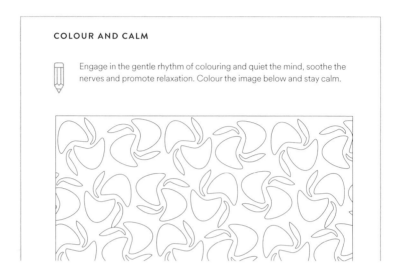

COLOUR AND CALM

Engage in the gentle rhythm of colouring and quiet the mind, soothe the nerves and promote relaxation. Colour the image below and stay calm.

WORK–LIFE BALANCE

Ever wondered if you are giving too much or not enough in your professional or personal life? Your planner will help you to visually see this on a regular basis.

At the end of every month of planning, you will fill in a work–life balance wheel. This concept was originally created by Paul J. Meyer and is a fantastic visual tool to see how your life is balanced and whether there are any areas you can improve on.

Here, this wheel is split into two halves – work and life – and you can see eight key areas in a single snapshot.

Once you have filled it in, take a moment to reflect. Are you giving too much or too little to any areas? How does it make you feel? How can you do better? Use the space around the wheel to note ways in which you can add more balance to your work and life. The wheel is something you can look back on and reflect upon, serving as a valuable visual tool.

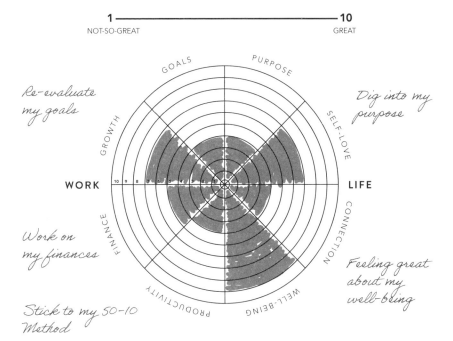

1 ———————————————— 10
NOT-SO-GREAT   GREAT

GOALS   PURPOSE
GROWTH   SELF-LOVE
WORK   LIFE
FINANCE   CONNECTION
PRODUCTIVITY   WELL-BEING

Re-evaluate my goals

Dig into my purpose

Work on my finances

Feeling great about my well-being

Stick to my 50-10 Method

MONTHLY REVIEW

Perfection does not exist, but you can strive to improve with each passing day and week. Self-reflection is essential, as it reveals areas of strength and areas needing attention. Every thirty days, you will be prompted with specific questions to reflect on the past few weeks, identify areas for improvement and plan for progress moving forward.

ROUTINE

How to create a positive daily structure that works for you

Having a routine adds structure to your day, helping you to be more productive and focused. You do not need to overthink or complicate your routine – simplicity is key. If you wish, you can slowly add to your routine over time by habit stacking, working with what benefits you most.

 ## MY MORNING ROUTINE

What you do first thing in the morning can help set the tone for the rest of your day. Incorporating healthy habits such as making your bed, meditating or journaling can kickstart your day positively and cultivate a more productive and fulfilling day that aligns with your goals.

Establish your morning routine below:

MY MORNING ROUTINE

TIME

MY EVENING ROUTINE

Your evening routine, or wind-down hour, is just as important as your morning routine, as it allows your mind and body to slow down. Doing something as simple as reading a book for twenty minutes every evening, staying away from screens or doing evening stretches will help you switch off for the day, leading to a great night's sleep.

Establish your evening routine below:

MY EVENING ROUTINE

TIME	

MY PLANNER

LIFE WILL TEST ME JUST BEFORE IT WILL BLESS ME

SLEEP TRACKER

MOOD TRACKER

WATER TRACKER

5.00	
5.30	
6.00	
6.30	
7.00	
7.30	
8.00	
8.30	
9.00	
9.30	
10.00	
10.30	
11.00	
11.30	
12.00	
12.30	
13.00	
13.30	
14.00	
13.30	
15.00	
15.30	
16.00	
16.30	
17.00	
17.30	
18.00	
18.30	
19.00	
19.30	
20.00	
20.30	
21.00	
21.30	
22.00	

POWER HOUR

50-10 METHOD

1. _____
2. _____
3. _____
4. _____
5. _____

NOTES

Scan to meditate:

One moment I want to remember from today is . . .

What am I grateful for?

I have looked after myself today by . . .

GRATITUDE IS THE GIFT THAT KEEPS ON GIVING

SLEEP TRACKER   MOOD TRACKER   WATER TRACKER

5.00	POWER HOUR
5.30	○
6.00	○
6.30	○
7.00	○
7.30	○
8.00	○
8.30	○
9.00	○
9.30	○
10.00	○
10.30	○
11.00	○
11.30	○
12.00	○
12.30	
13.00	
13.30	
14.00	
13.30	
15.00	
15.30	
16.00	
16.30	
17.00	**50-10 METHOD**
17.30	
18.00	1. ○
18.30	
19.00	2. ○
19.30	3. ○
20.00	
20.30	4. ○
21.00	
21.30	5. ○
22.00	

NOTES

Scan to meditate:

One moment I want to remember from today is . . .

_____

_____

What made me smile today?

_____

_____

I have looked after myself today by . . .

_____

_____

I AM FOCUSED ON MY GOALS, MY MINDSET AND MY HAPPINESS

SLEEP TRACKER

MOOD TRACKER

WATER TRACKER

	POWER HOUR
5.00	
5.30	○
6.00	○
6.30	○
7.00	○
7.30	○
8.00	○
8.30	○
9.00	○
9.30	○
10.00	○
10.30	○
11.00	○
11.30	
12.00	
12.30	
13.00	
13.30	
14.00	
13.30	
15.00	
15.30	
16.00	
16.30	
17.00	**50-10 METHOD**
17.30	
18.00	1. ○
18.30	
19.00	2. ○
19.30	3. ○
20.00	
20.30	4. ○
21.00	
21.30	5. ○
22.00	

NOTES

Scan to meditate:

One moment I want to remember from today is . . .

_____

_____

What brought me joy today?

_____

_____

I have looked after myself today by . . .

_____

_____

I WILL NOT LET FEAR KEEP ME FROM TRYING

SLEEP TRACKER   MOOD TRACKER   WATER TRACKER

Time		POWER HOUR
5.00		○
5.30		○
6.00		○
6.30		○
7.00		○
7.30		○
8.00		○
8.30		○
9.00		○
9.30		○
10.00		○
10.30		○
11.00		○
11.30		
12.00		
12.30		
13.00		
13.30		
14.00		50-10 METHOD
13.30		
15.00		1. ○
15.30		2. ○
16.00		3. ○
16.30		4. ○
17.00		5. ○
17.30		
18.00		
18.30		
19.00		
19.30		
20.00		
20.30		
21.00		
21.30		
22.00		

NOTES

Scan to meditate:

One moment I want to remember from today is . . .

How have I been blessed today?

I have looked after myself today by . . .

I LOVE MYSELF UNCONDITIONALLY

SLEEP TRACKER	MOOD TRACKER	WATER TRACKER
☽ ☽ ☽ ☽ ☽ ☽ ☽	☺ ☺ ☺ ☺ ☺ ☺	▯ ▯ ▯ ▯ ▯ ▯ ▯ ▯

	POWER HOUR
5.00	○
5.30	
6.00	○
6.30	
7.00	○
7.30	
8.00	○
8.30	
9.00	○
9.30	
10.00	○
10.30	
11.00	○
11.30	
12.00	○
12.30	
13.00	○
13.30	
14.00	○
13.30	
15.00	○
15.30	
16.00	
16.30	
17.00	**50-10 METHOD**
17.30	
18.00	1. ○
18.30	
19.00	2. ○
19.30	
20.00	3. ○
20.30	
21.00	4. ○
21.30	
22.00	5. ○

NOTES

Scan to
meditate:

One moment I want to remember from today is . . .

In what ways did I receive help today?

I have looked after myself today by . . .

I COUNT MY BLESSINGS, TODAY AND EVERY DAY

SATURDAY LIST

1. _____ ○
2. _____ ○
3. _____ ○
4. _____ ○
5. _____ ○

SUNDAY LIST

1. _____ ○
2. _____ ○
3. _____ ○
4. _____ ○
5. _____ ○

DIGITAL DETOX   SELF-CARE SUNDAY   HAVE FUN

GOALS FOR NEXT WEEK

_____

_____

_____

_____

MIND DUMP

Q&A: SELF-DISCOVERY

Take the first step on your path of self-discovery with these empowering journal prompts. Dive in and unlock the depth of your inner wisdom.

WHAT MAKES ME FEEL MOST ALIVE AND PRESENT IN THE MOMENT?

HOW HAS MY LAST ACHIEVEMENT MADE ME FEEL?

DESCRIBE A PEACEFUL PLACE AND WHY IT RESONATES WITH ME:

HOW DID I COPE AND LEARN FROM A PAST CHALLENGE?

HOW CAN I ADAPT THE TRAITS I ADMIRE MOST IN OTHERS?

I RELEASE THE OUTCOME AND TRUST THE PROCESS

SLEEP TRACKER	MOOD TRACKER	WATER TRACKER
🌙 🌙 🌙 🌙 🌙 🌙 🌙 🌙	☺ ☺ ☺ ☺ ☺	▯ ▯ ▯ ▯ ▯ ▯ ▯ ▯

	POWER HOUR
5.00	
5.30	○
6.00	○
6.30	○
7.00	○
7.30	○
8.00	○
8.30	○
9.00	○
9.30	○
10.00	○
10.30	○
11.00	○
11.30	○
12.00	○
12.30	
13.00	
13.30	
14.00	
13.30	
15.00	
15.30	
16.00	
16.30	
17.00	**50-10 METHOD**
17.30	
18.00	1. ___ ○
18.30	2. ___ ○
19.00	3. ___ ○
19.30	4. ___ ○
20.00	5. ___ ○
20.30	
21.00	
21.30	
22.00	

NOTES

Scan to meditate:

One moment I want to remember from today is . . .

Who am I most thankful for today?

I have looked after myself today by . . .

REMINDER: I AM WORTHY OF SO MUCH MORE

SLEEP TRACKER

MOOD TRACKER

WATER TRACKER

Time	
5.00	
5.30	
6.00	
6.30	
7.00	
7.30	
8.00	
8.30	
9.00	
9.30	
10.00	
10.30	
11.00	
11.30	
12.00	
12.30	
13.00	
13.30	
14.00	
13.30	
15.00	
15.30	
16.00	
16.30	
17.00	
17.30	
18.00	
18.30	
19.00	
19.30	
20.00	
20.30	
21.00	
21.30	
22.00	

POWER HOUR

50-10 METHOD

1.
2.
3.
4.
5.

NOTES

Scan to
meditate:

One moment I want to remember from today is . . .

_____

_____

What is something that cheered me up today?

_____

_____

I have looked after myself today by . . .

_____

_____

I CHOOSE TO BE AROUND PEOPLE WHO
FIT MY FUTURE, NOT MY PAST

SLEEP TRACKER   MOOD TRACKER   WATER TRACKER

| 5.00 |
| 5.30 |
| 6.00 |
| 6.30 |
| 7.00 |
| 7.30 |
| 8.00 |
| 8.30 |
| 9.00 |
| 9.30 |
| 10.00 |
| 10.30 |
| 11.00 |
| 11.30 |
| 12.00 |
| 12.30 |
| 13.00 |
| 13.30 |
| 14.00 |
| 13.30 |
| 15.00 |
| 15.30 |
| 16.00 |
| 16.30 |
| 17.00 |
| 17.30 |
| 18.00 |
| 18.30 |
| 19.00 |
| 19.30 |
| 20.00 |
| 20.30 |
| 21.00 |
| 21.30 |
| 22.00 |

POWER HOUR

○ _____
○ _____
○ _____
○ _____
○ _____
○ _____
○ _____
○ _____
○ _____
○ _____
○ _____
○ _____

50-10 METHOD

1. _____ ○
2. _____ ○
3. _____ ○
4. _____ ○
5. _____ ○

NOTES

Scan to meditate:

One moment I want to remember from today is . . .

What was one thing that made me happy today?

I have looked after myself today by . . .

IT IS NEVER TOO LATE: I CAN START TODAY

SLEEP TRACKER   MOOD TRACKER   WATER TRACKER

5.00	....
5.30	....
6.00	....
6.30	....
7.00	....
7.30	....
8.00	....
8.30	....
9.00	....
9.30	....
10.00	....
10.30	....
11.00	....
11.30	....
12.00	....
12.30	....
13.00	....
13.30	....
14.00	....
13.30	....
15.00	....
15.30	....
16.00	....
16.30	....
17.00	....
17.30	....
18.00	....
18.30	....
19.00	....
19.30	....
20.00	....
20.30	....
21.00	....
21.30	....
22.00	....

POWER HOUR

○ _____
○ _____
○ _____
○ _____
○ _____
○ _____
○ _____
○ _____
○ _____
○ _____
○ _____
○ _____

50-10 METHOD

1. _____ ○
2. _____ ○
3. _____ ○
4. _____ ○
5. _____ ○

NOTES

Scan to
meditate:

One moment I want to remember from today is . . .

How can I spread kindness tomorrow?

I have looked after myself today by . . .

I WILL ENJOY THE JOURNEY – IT MIGHT JUST CHANGE MY LIFE

SLEEP TRACKER

☽ ☽ ☽ ☽ ☽ ☽ ☽ ☽

MOOD TRACKER

☺ ☺ ☺ ☺ ☺

WATER TRACKER

▯ ▯ ▯ ▯ ▯ ▯ ▯ ▯

	POWER HOUR
5.00	
5.30	
6.00	○
6.30	○
7.00	○
7.30	○
8.00	○
8.30	○
9.00	○
9.30	○
10.00	○
10.30	○
11.00	○
11.30	○
12.00	○
12.30	○
13.00	○
13.30	○
14.00	○
13.30	○
15.00	○
15.30	
16.00	
16.30	
17.00	
17.30	**50-10 METHOD**
18.00	1. ○
18.30	2. ○
19.00	3. ○
19.30	4. ○
20.00	5. ○
20.30	
21.00	
21.30	
22.00	

NOTES

Scan to
meditate:

One moment I want to remember from today is . . .

_____

_____

What is something that I accomplished today?

_____

_____

I have looked after myself today by . . .

_____

_____

REMINDER: IF I BELIEVE I DESERVE IT, IT WILL BE MINE

SATURDAY LIST

1. _____ ○
2. _____ ○
3. _____ ○
4. _____ ○
5. _____ ○

SUNDAY LIST

1. _____ ○
2. _____ ○
3. _____ ○
4. _____ ○
5. _____ ○

DIGITAL DETOX ●   SELF-CARE SUNDAY ●   HAVE FUN ●

GOALS FOR NEXT WEEK

_____

_____

_____

_____

_____

MIND DUMP

COLOUR AND CALM

Engage in the gentle rhythm of colouring and quiet the mind, soothe the nerves and promote relaxation. Colour the image below and stay calm.

WHEN I ALIGN WITH MY PURPOSE, EVERYTHING FALLS INTO PLACE

SLEEP TRACKER   MOOD TRACKER   WATER TRACKER

5.00		POWER HOUR
5.30		
6.00	○	
6.30		
7.00	○	
7.30		
8.00	○	
8.30		
9.00	○	
9.30		
10.00	○	
10.30		
11.00	○	
11.30		
12.00	○	
12.30		
13.00	○	
13.30		
14.00	○	
13.30		
15.00	○	
15.30		
16.00		
16.30		
17.00		**50-10 METHOD**
17.30		
18.00		1. ○
18.30		
19.00		2. ○
19.30		
20.00		3. ○
20.30		
21.00		4. ○
21.30		
22.00		5. ○

NOTES

Scan to meditate:

One moment I want to remember from today is . . .

What is a strength of mine that I utilize every day?

I have looked after myself today by . . .

I AM NOT BEHIND, I AM ON MY OWN BEAUTIFUL PATH

SLEEP TRACKER   MOOD TRACKER   WATER TRACKER

5.00
5.30
6.00
6.30
7.00
7.30
8.00
8.30
9.00
9.30
10.00
10.30
11.00
11.30
12.00
12.30
13.00
13.30
14.00
13.30
15.00
15.30
16.00
16.30
17.00
17.30
18.00
18.30
19.00
19.30
20.00
20.30
21.00
21.30
22.00

POWER HOUR

50-10 METHOD

1.
2.
3.
4.
5.

NOTES

Scan to
meditate:

One moment I want to remember from today is . . .

What is one thing I did today that made me proud of myself?

I have looked after myself today by . . .

I CREATE MY FUTURE WITH EVERY LITTLE STEP I TAKE

SLEEP TRACKER   MOOD TRACKER   WATER TRACKER

POWER HOUR

5.00
5.30
6.00
6.30
7.00
7.30
8.00
8.30
9.00
9.30
10.00
10.30
11.00
11.30
12.00
12.30
13.00
13.30
14.00
13.30
15.00
15.30
16.00
16.30
17.00
17.30
18.00
18.30
19.00
19.30
20.00
20.30
21.00
21.30
22.00

50-10 METHOD

1.
2.
3.
4.
5.

NOTES

Scan to
meditate:

One moment I want to remember from today is . . .

_____

_____

What small act of kindness did I witness today?

_____

_____

I have looked after myself today by . . .

_____

_____

NOTHING CAN STOP ME ACHIEVING MY DREAMS

SLEEP TRACKER   MOOD TRACKER   WATER TRACKER

5.00	
5.30	POWER HOUR
6.00	○
6.30	○
7.00	○
7.30	○
8.00	○
8.30	○
9.00	○
9.30	○
10.00	○
10.30	○
11.00	○
11.30	○
12.00	○
12.30	
13.00	
13.30	
14.00	
13.30	
15.00	
15.30	
16.00	
16.30	
17.00	50-10 METHOD
17.30	
18.00	1. _____ ○
18.30	
19.00	2. _____ ○
19.30	
20.00	3. _____ ○
20.30	
21.00	4. _____ ○
21.30	
22.00	5. _____ ○

NOTES

Scan to
meditate:

One moment I want to remember from today is . . .

_____

_____

What made me feel inspired today?

_____

_____

I have looked after myself today by . . .

_____

_____

I WILL SHOW UP FOR MYSELF BEFORE I SHOW UP FOR OTHERS

SLEEP TRACKER

☾ ☾ ☾ ☾ ☾ ☾ ☾ ☾

MOOD TRACKER

☺ ☺ ☺ ☺ ☺

WATER TRACKER

▢ ▢ ▢ ▢ ▢ ▢ ▢ ▢

5.00	
5.30	
6.00	
6.30	
7.00	
7.30	
8.00	
8.30	
9.00	
9.30	
10.00	
10.30	
11.00	
11.30	
12.00	
12.30	
13.00	
13.30	
14.00	
13.30	
15.00	
15.30	
16.00	
16.30	
17.00	
17.30	
18.00	
18.30	
19.00	
19.30	
20.00	
20.30	
21.00	
21.30	
22.00	

POWER HOUR

○ _____
○ _____
○ _____
○ _____
○ _____
○ _____
○ _____
○ _____
○ _____
○ _____
○ _____
○ _____

50-10 METHOD

1. _____ ○
2. _____ ○
3. _____ ○
4. _____ ○
5. _____ ○

NOTES

Scan to
meditate:

One moment I want to remember from today is . . .

_____

_____

How did I experience peace today?

_____

_____

I have looked after myself today by . . .

_____

_____

THIS IS MY TIME TO SHINE

SATURDAY LIST

1. _____ ○
2. _____ ○
3. _____ ○
4. _____ ○
5. _____ ○

SUNDAY LIST

1. _____ ○
2. _____ ○
3. _____ ○
4. _____ ○
5. _____ ○

DIGITAL DETOX ○   SELF-CARE SUNDAY ○   HAVE FUN ○

GOALS FOR NEXT WEEK

_____

_____

_____

_____

_____

MIND DUMP

ABOUT ME

One of the most important relationships you will ever have is the one you have with yourself. Take the time to truly understand and connect with who you are by answering the questions below.

WHAT MOTIVATES ME?

MY GOOD HABITS ARE:

HABITS I NEED TO WORK ON:

MY TOP THREE GOALS ARE:

I WILL NOT GIVE UP. GOOD IS ON THE WAY

SLEEP TRACKER   MOOD TRACKER   WATER TRACKER

5.00	....
5.30	....
6.00	....
6.30	....
7.00	....
7.30	....
8.00	....
8.30	....
9.00	....
9.30	....
10.00	....
10.30	....
11.00	....
11.30	....
12.00	....
12.30	....
13.00	....
13.30	....
14.00	....
13.30	....
15.00	....
15.30	....
16.00	....
16.30	....
17.00	....
17.30	....
18.00	....
18.30	....
19.00	....
19.30	....
20.00	....
20.30	....
21.00	....
21.30	....
22.00	....

POWER HOUR

○ _____
○ _____
○ _____
○ _____
○ _____
○ _____
○ _____
○ _____
○ _____
○ _____
○ _____
○ _____

50-10 METHOD

1. _____ ○
2. _____ ○
3. _____ ○
4. _____ ○
5. _____ ○

NOTES

Scan to
meditate:

One moment I want to remember from today is . . .

_____

_____

What made me appreciate the present moment today?

_____

_____

I have looked after myself today by . . .

_____

_____

REMINDER: I WILL NOT LOOK BACK. I AM NOT GOING THAT WAY

SLEEP TRACKER	MOOD TRACKER	WATER TRACKER
☽ ☽ ☽ ☽ ☽ ☽ ☽ ☽	☺ ☺ ☺ ☺ ☺	▭ ▭ ▭ ▭ ▭ ▭ ▭ ▭

5.00	**POWER HOUR**
5.30	
6.00	○ _____
6.30	○ _____
7.00	○ _____
7.30	○ _____
8.00	○ _____
8.30	○ _____
9.00	○ _____
9.30	○ _____
10.00	○ _____
10.30	○ _____
11.00	○ _____
11.30	○ _____
12.00	○ _____
12.30	○ _____
13.00	
13.30	
14.00	
13.30	
15.00	
15.30	
16.00	
16.30	**50-10 METHOD**
17.00	
17.30	1. _____ ○
18.00	2. _____ ○
18.30	3. _____ ○
19.00	4. _____ ○
19.30	5. _____ ○
20.00	
20.30	
21.00	
21.30	
22.00	

NOTES

Scan to
meditate:

One moment I want to remember from today is . . .

_____

_____

How did I praise myself today?

_____

_____

I have looked after myself today by . . .

_____

_____

REJECTION IS THE UNIVERSE REDIRECTING ME TO MY DREAMS

SLEEP TRACKER   MOOD TRACKER   WATER TRACKER

5.00	....
5.30	....
6.00	....
6.30	....
7.00	....
7.30	....
8.00	....
8.30	....
9.00	....
9.30	....
10.00	....
10.30	....
11.00	....
11.30	....
12.00	....
12.30	....
13.00	....
13.30	....
14.00	....
13.30	....
15.00	....
15.30	....
16.00	....
16.30	....
17.00	....
17.30	....
18.00	....
18.30	....
19.00	....
19.30	....
20.00	....
20.30	....
21.00	....
21.30	....
22.00	....

POWER HOUR

○ _____
○ _____
○ _____
○ _____
○ _____
○ _____
○ _____
○ _____
○ _____
○ _____
○ _____
○ _____

50-10 METHOD

1. _____ ○
2. _____ ○
3. _____ ○
4. _____ ○
5. _____ ○

NOTES

Scan to
meditate:

One moment I want to remember from today is . . .

_____

_____

How did I spend time doing what I love today?

_____

_____

I have looked after myself today by . . .

_____

_____

I CHOOSE TO RESPOND INSTEAD OF REACT

SLEEP TRACKER   MOOD TRACKER   WATER TRACKER

5.00	....
5.30	....
6.00	....
6.30	....
7.00	....
7.30	....
8.00	....
8.30	....
9.00	....
9.30	....
10.00	....
10.30	....
11.00	....
11.30	....
12.00	....
12.30	....
13.00	....
13.30	....
14.00	....
13.30	....
15.00	....
15.30	....
16.00	....
16.30	....
17.00	....
17.30	....
18.00	....
18.30	....
19.00	....
19.30	....
20.00	....
20.30	....
21.00	....
21.30	....
22.00	....

POWER HOUR

○ _____
○ _____
○ _____
○ _____
○ _____
○ _____
○ _____
○ _____
○ _____
○ _____
○ _____
○ _____

50-10 METHOD

1. _____ ○
2. _____ ○
3. _____ ○
4. _____ ○
5. _____ ○

NOTES

Scan to
meditate:

One moment I want to remember from today is . . .

What good news did I receive today?

I have looked after myself today by . . .

I WORK WITH HEART. I WALK WITH FAITH. LET THE UNIVERSE HANDLE IT

SLEEP TRACKER   MOOD TRACKER   WATER TRACKER

5.00	
5.30	
6.00	
6.30	
7.00	
7.30	
8.00	
8.30	
9.00	
9.30	
10.00	
10.30	
11.00	
11.30	
12.00	
12.30	
13.00	
13.30	
14.00	
13.30	
15.00	
15.30	
16.00	
16.30	
17.00	
17.30	
18.00	
18.30	
19.00	
19.30	
20.00	
20.30	
21.00	
21.30	
22.00	

POWER HOUR

50-10 METHOD

1.
2.
3.
4.
5.

NOTES

Scan to meditate:

One moment I want to remember from today is . . .

Who brought me joy today?

I have looked after myself today by . . .

THE CALMER I FEEL, THE CLEARER I WILL THINK

SATURDAY LIST

1. _____ ○
2. _____ ○
3. _____ ○
4. _____ ○
5. _____ ○

SUNDAY LIST

1. _____ ○
2. _____ ○
3. _____ ○
4. _____ ○
5. _____ ○

DIGITAL DETOX ●   SELF-CARE SUNDAY ●   HAVE FUN ●

GOALS FOR NEXT WEEK

_____

_____

_____

_____

_____

MIND DUMP

MINDFUL CHALLENGE

 Challenge yourself to be more mindful. Tick any of the below that you have managed to do recently. One is left blank for you to fill in with something that is personal to you.

BE GRATEFUL
FOR ONE
THING TODAY

STAY AWAY FROM
YOUR PHONE
FOR TWO HOURS

HAVE A MINDFUL MEAL

JOURNAL YOUR
THOUGHTS

TAKE THREE LONG,
DEEP BREATHS

ENJOY FRESH
MORNING AIR

MY MONTHLY WORK–LIFE BALANCE WHEEL

 On a scale of 1 to 10, how am I feeling in the following areas of my work and life? Do not overthink it, just colour it in!

1 ———————————————————————— **10**
NOT-SO-GREAT   GREAT

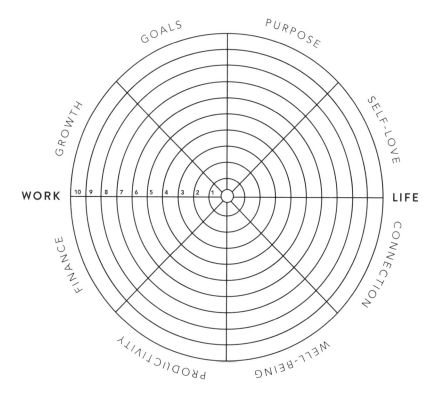

 Tip: Use the space around the wheel to note ways in which you can add more balance to your life.

MY MONTHLY REVIEW

WHAT WENT WELL THIS MONTH?

DID I STRUGGLE WITH ANYTHING THIS MONTH?

IS THERE ANYTHING I COULD HAVE DONE DIFFERENTLY?

WHAT THREE EMOTIONS RULED MY ENERGY THIS MONTH?

HOW CAN I ADD MORE BALANCE INTO MY LIFE GOING FORWARD?

WHAT IS ONE THING I WANT TO START/DO/ACHIEVE NEXT MONTH?

WITHOUT DISCIPLINE, THERE IS NO ROAD TO SUCCESS

SLEEP TRACKER   MOOD TRACKER   WATER TRACKER

| 5.00 |
| 5.30 |
| 6.00 |
| 6.30 |
| 7.00 |
| 7.30 |
| 8.00 |
| 8.30 |
| 9.00 |
| 9.30 |
| 10.00 |
| 10.30 |
| 11.00 |
| 11.30 |
| 12.00 |
| 12.30 |
| 13.00 |
| 13.30 |
| 14.00 |
| 13.30 |
| 15.00 |
| 15.30 |
| 16.00 |
| 16.30 |
| 17.00 |
| 17.30 |
| 18.00 |
| 18.30 |
| 19.00 |
| 19.30 |
| 20.00 |
| 20.30 |
| 21.00 |
| 21.30 |
| 22.00 |

POWER HOUR

○ _____
○ _____
○ _____
○ _____
○ _____
○ _____
○ _____
○ _____
○ _____
○ _____
○ _____
○ _____

50-10 METHOD

1. _____ ○
2. _____ ○
3. _____ ○
4. _____ ○
5. _____ ○

NOTES

Scan to meditate:

One moment I want to remember from today is . . .

_____

_____

How have I grown as a person recently?

_____

_____

I have looked after myself today by . . .

_____

_____

THE CHOICE IS MINE. I WILL MAKE IT HAPPEN TODAY

SLEEP TRACKER   MOOD TRACKER   WATER TRACKER

🌙 🌙 🌙 🌙 🌙 🌙 🌙 🌙   ☺ ☺ ☺ ☺ ☺   ▯ ▯ ▯ ▯ ▯ ▯ ▯ ▯

Time	
5.00	
5.30	
6.00	
6.30	
7.00	
7.30	
8.00	
8.30	
9.00	
9.30	
10.00	
10.30	
11.00	
11.30	
12.00	
12.30	
13.00	
13.30	
14.00	
13.30	
15.00	
15.30	
16.00	
16.30	
17.00	
17.30	
18.00	
18.30	
19.00	
19.30	
20.00	
20.30	
21.00	
21.30	
22.00	

POWER HOUR

○ _____
○ _____
○ _____
○ _____
○ _____
○ _____
○ _____
○ _____
○ _____
○ _____
○ _____

50-10 METHOD

1. _____ ○
2. _____ ○
3. _____ ○
4. _____ ○
5. _____ ○

NOTES

Scan to meditate:

One moment I want to remember from today is . . .

What positive habits am I developing?

I have looked after myself today by . . .

I WILL NOT FORGET TO LIVE WITH INTENTION

SLEEP TRACKER	MOOD TRACKER	WATER TRACKER
☾ ☾ ☾ ☾ ☾ ☾ ☾	☺ ☺ ☺ ☺ ☺	▯ ▯ ▯ ▯ ▯ ▯ ▯ ▯

5.00
5.30
6.00
6.30
7.00
7.30
8.00
8.30
9.00
9.30
10.00
10.30
11.00
11.30
12.00
12.30
13.00
13.30
14.00
13.30
15.00
15.30
16.00
16.30
17.00
17.30
18.00
18.30
19.00
19.30
20.00
20.30
21.00
21.30
22.00

POWER HOUR

○
○
○
○
○
○
○
○
○
○
○
○
○

50-10 METHOD

1. _____ ○
2. _____ ○
3. _____ ○
4. _____ ○
5. _____ ○

NOTES

Scan to meditate:

One moment I want to remember from today is . . .

_____

_____

What makes me unique?

_____

_____

I have looked after myself today by . . .

_____

_____

I INHALE CALM. I EXHALE WORRY

SLEEP TRACKER   MOOD TRACKER   WATER TRACKER

5.00	
5.30	
6.00	
6.30	
7.00	
7.30	
8.00	
8.30	
9.00	
9.30	
10.00	
10.30	
11.00	
11.30	
12.00	
12.30	
13.00	
13.30	
14.00	
13.30	
15.00	
15.30	
16.00	
16.30	
17.00	
17.30	
18.00	
18.30	
19.00	
19.30	
20.00	
20.30	
21.00	
21.30	
22.00	

POWER HOUR

50-10 METHOD

1.
2.
3.
4.
5.

NOTES

Scan to
meditate:

One moment I want to remember from today is . . .

What is a small goal that I achieved today?

I have looked after myself today by . . .

REMINDER: MY LIFE IS AS GOOD AS MY MINDSET

SLEEP TRACKER 　　　 MOOD TRACKER 　　　 WATER TRACKER

☾ ☾ ☾ ☾ ☾ ☾ ☾ ☾ 　 ☺ ☺ ☺ ☺ ☺ 　 ▯ ▯ ▯ ▯ ▯ ▯ ▯ ▯

Time		POWER HOUR
5.00		
5.30		○
6.00		○
6.30		○
7.00		○
7.30		○
8.00		○
8.30		○
9.00		○
9.30		○
10.00		○
10.30		○
11.00		○
11.30		○
12.00		
12.30		
13.00		
13.30		
14.00		
13.30		
15.00		
15.30		
16.00		
16.30		
17.00		50-10 METHOD
17.30		
18.00		1. ○
18.30		2. ○
19.00		3. ○
19.30		4. ○
20.00		5. ○
20.30		
21.00		
21.30		
22.00		

NOTES

Scan to
meditate:

One moment I want to remember from today is . . .

How can I show someone else love tomorrow?

I have looked after myself today by . . .

I CELEBRATE MY PROGRESS, NO MATTER HOW BIG OR SMALL

SATURDAY LIST

1. _____ ○
2. _____ ○
3. _____ ○
4. _____ ○
5. _____ ○

SUNDAY LIST

1. _____ ○
2. _____ ○
3. _____ ○
4. _____ ○
5. _____ ○

DIGITAL DETOX ●   SELF-CARE SUNDAY ●   HAVE FUN ●

GOALS FOR NEXT WEEK

_____
_____
_____
_____

MIND DUMP

WRITE AND RELEASE

There is power in putting pen to paper and releasing any thoughts and emotions, both good and bad, that you may be feeling. Whatever is on your mind, write it out and let it go.

I AM DOING GREAT. I WILL NEVER FORGET THAT

SLEEP TRACKER	MOOD TRACKER	WATER TRACKER

5.00

5.30

6.00

6.30

7.00

7.30

8.00

8.30

9.00

9.30

10.00

10.30

11.00

11.30

12.00

12.30

13.00

13.30

14.00

13.30

15.00

15.30

16.00

16.30

17.00

17.30

18.00

18.30

19.00

19.30

20.00

20.30

21.00

21.30

22.00

POWER HOUR

○

○

○

○

○

○

○

○

○

○

○

50-10 METHOD

1. _____ ○

2. _____ ○

3. _____ ○

4. _____ ○

5. _____ ○

NOTES

Scan to meditate:

One moment I want to remember from today is . . .

Someone that inspires me is...

I have looked after myself today by . . .

REMINDER: I WILL NEVER DOUBT MY VISION

SLEEP TRACKER
☽ ☽ ☽ ☽ ☽ ☽ ☽ ☽

MOOD TRACKER
☺ ☺ ☺ ☺ ☺

WATER TRACKER
▢ ▢ ▢ ▢ ▢ ▢ ▢ ▢

Time	
5.00	
5.30	
6.00	
6.30	
7.00	
7.30	
8.00	
8.30	
9.00	
9.30	
10.00	
10.30	
11.00	
11.30	
12.00	
12.30	
13.00	
13.30	
14.00	
13.30	
15.00	
15.30	
16.00	
16.30	
17.00	
17.30	
18.00	
18.30	
19.00	
19.30	
20.00	
20.30	
21.00	
21.30	
22.00	

POWER HOUR

○
○
○
○
○
○
○
○
○
○
○
○

50-10 METHOD

1. _____ ○
2. _____ ○
3. _____ ○
4. _____ ○
5. _____ ○

NOTES

Scan to meditate:

One moment I want to remember from today is . . .

_____

_____

Who is someone I can message or call to tell them I love them?

_____

_____

I have looked after myself today by . . .

_____

_____

I AM WHAT I READ, SPEAK, WATCH, HEAR, THINK AND FEEL

SLEEP TRACKER   MOOD TRACKER   WATER TRACKER

	POWER HOUR
5.00	○
5.30	○
6.00	○
6.30	○
7.00	○
7.30	○
8.00	○
8.30	○
9.00	○
9.30	○
10.00	○
10.30	○
11.00	○
11.30	
12.00	
12.30	
13.00	
13.30	
14.00	
13.30	
15.00	

POWER HOUR

○ ———
○ ———
○ ———
○ ———
○ ———
○ ———
○ ———
○ ———
○ ———
○ ———
○ ———
○ ———

15.30
16.00
16.30
17.00
17.30
18.00
18.30
19.00
19.30
20.00
20.30
21.00
21.30
22.00

50-10 METHOD

1. _____ ○
2. _____ ○
3. _____ ○
4. _____ ○
5. _____ ○

NOTES

Scan to
meditate:

One moment I want to remember from today is . . .

_____

_____

What is something I love about my home?

_____

_____

I have looked after myself today by . . .

_____

_____

I WILL STAY PATIENT, STAY POSITIVE AND KEEP PUSHING FORWARD

SLEEP TRACKER	MOOD TRACKER	WATER TRACKER
☽ ☽ ☽ ☽ ☽ ☽ ☽ ☽	☺ ☺ ☺ ☺ ☺	▭ ▭ ▭ ▭ ▭ ▭ ▭ ▭

5.00	**POWER HOUR**
5.30	○ _____
6.00	○ _____
6.30	○ _____
7.00	○ _____
7.30	○ _____
8.00	○ _____
8.30	○ _____
9.00	○ _____
9.30	○ _____
10.00	○ _____
10.30	○ _____
11.00	○ _____
11.30	○ _____
12.00	○ _____
12.30	
13.00	
13.30	
14.00	
13.30	
15.00	
15.30	**50-10 METHOD**
16.00	
16.30	
17.00	1. _____ ○
17.30	
18.00	2. _____ ○
18.30	
19.00	3. _____ ○
19.30	
20.00	4. _____ ○
20.30	
21.00	5. _____ ○
21.30	
22.00	

NOTES

Scan to meditate:

One moment I want to remember from today is . . .

How can I make someone else's day better?

I have looked after myself today by . . .

I HAVE TO UNPLUG MYSELF IN ORDER TO RESET MYSELF

SLEEP TRACKER   MOOD TRACKER   WATER TRACKER

5.00
5.30
6.00
6.30
7.00
7.30
8.00
8.30
9.00
9.30
10.00
10.30
11.00
11.30
12.00
12.30
13.00
13.30
14.00
13.30
15.00
15.30
16.00
16.30
17.00
17.30
18.00
18.30
19.00
19.30
20.00
20.30
21.00
21.30
22.00

POWER HOUR

○
○
○
○
○
○
○
○
○
○
○
○

50-10 METHOD

1. ○
2. ○
3. ○
4. ○
5. ○

NOTES

Scan to meditate:

One moment I want to remember from today is . . .

_____

_____

How can I handle stress in a healthy way?

_____

_____

I have looked after myself today by . . .

_____

_____

IF I BELIEVE IN MYSELF, OTHERS WILL TOO

SATURDAY LIST

1. _____ ○
2. _____ ○
3. _____ ○
4. _____ ○
5. _____ ○

SUNDAY LIST

1. _____ ○
2. _____ ○
3. _____ ○
4. _____ ○
5. _____ ○

DIGITAL DETOX ●   SELF-CARE SUNDAY ●   HAVE FUN ●

GOALS FOR NEXT WEEK

_____

_____

_____

_____

MIND DUMP

COLOURING QUOTE

Colouring is a great way to get into a meditative state by calming the mind and feeling relaxed. Visualize and feel the words below as you colour.

I CHOOSE TO BE OPEN TO CHANGE, AS GROWTH ALWAYS FOLLOWS

SLEEP TRACKER	MOOD TRACKER	WATER TRACKER
☾ ☾ ☾ ☾ ☾ ☾ ☾ ☾	☺ ☺ ☺ ☺ ☺	▯ ▯ ▯ ▯ ▯ ▯ ▯ ▯

	POWER HOUR
5.00	○ _____
5.30	○ _____
6.00	○ _____
6.30	○ _____
7.00	○ _____
7.30	○ _____
8.00	○ _____
8.30	○ _____
9.00	○ _____
9.30	○ _____
10.00	○ _____
10.30	○ _____
11.00	
11.30	
12.00	
12.30	
13.00	
13.30	
14.00	
13.30	
15.00	
15.30	**50-10 METHOD**
16.00	
16.30	
17.00	
17.30	1. _____ ○
18.00	
18.30	2. _____ ○
19.00	
19.30	3. _____ ○
20.00	
20.30	4. _____ ○
21.00	
21.30	5. _____ ○
22.00	

NOTES

Scan to
meditate:

One moment I want to remember from today is . . .

What do I enjoy doing in my spare time?

I have looked after myself today by . . .

DISCIPLINE AND CONSISTENCY WILL GET ME TO MY GOALS

SLEEP TRACKER

☽ ☽ ☽ ☽ ☽ ☽ ☽ ☽

MOOD TRACKER

☺ ☺ ☺ ☺ ☺

WATER TRACKER

⬜ ⬜ ⬜ ⬜ ⬜ ⬜ ⬜ ⬜

Time	
5.00	
5.30	
6.00	
6.30	
7.00	
7.30	
8.00	
8.30	
9.00	
9.30	
10.00	
10.30	
11.00	
11.30	
12.00	
12.30	
13.00	
13.30	
14.00	
13.30	
15.00	
15.30	
16.00	
16.30	
17.00	
17.30	
18.00	
18.30	
19.00	
19.30	
20.00	
20.30	
21.00	
21.30	
22.00	

POWER HOUR

○ _____
○ _____
○ _____
○ _____
○ _____
○ _____
○ _____
○ _____
○ _____
○ _____
○ _____
○ _____

50-10 METHOD

1. _____ ○
2. _____ ○
3. _____ ○
4. _____ ○
5. _____ ○

NOTES

Scan to meditate:

One moment I want to remember from today is . . .

A positive affirmation to help me right now is:

I have looked after myself today by . . .

IT IS OK TO MAKE MISTAKES AND LEARN FROM THEM

SLEEP TRACKER

🌙 🌙 🌙 🌙 🌙 🌙 🌙

MOOD TRACKER

☺ ☺ ☺ ☺ ☺

WATER TRACKER

▯ ▯ ▯ ▯ ▯ ▯ ▯ ▯

5.00	
5.30	
6.00	
6.30	
7.00	
7.30	
8.00	
8.30	
9.00	
9.30	
10.00	
10.30	
11.00	
11.30	
12.00	
12.30	
13.00	
13.30	
14.00	
13.30	
15.00	
15.30	
16.00	
16.30	
17.00	
17.30	
18.00	
18.30	
19.00	
19.30	
20.00	
20.30	
21.00	
21.30	
22.00	

POWER HOUR

○ _____
○ _____
○ _____
○ _____
○ _____
○ _____
○ _____
○ _____
○ _____
○ _____
○ _____

50-10 METHOD

1. _____ ○
2. _____ ○
3. _____ ○
4. _____ ○
5. _____ ○

NOTES

Scan to
meditate:

One moment I want to remember from today is . . .

What energizes me?

I have looked after myself today by . . .

ACTION, DEDICATION AND ROUTINE WILL ALWAYS LEAD TO GROWTH

SLEEP TRACKER

🌙 🌙 🌙 🌙 🌙 🌙 🌙 🌙

MOOD TRACKER

☺ ☺ ☺ ☺ ☺

WATER TRACKER

⬜ ⬜ ⬜ ⬜ ⬜ ⬜ ⬜ ⬜

Time	
5.00	
5.30	
6.00	
6.30	
7.00	
7.30	
8.00	
8.30	
9.00	
9.30	
10.00	
10.30	
11.00	
11.30	
12.00	
12.30	
13.00	
13.30	
14.00	
13.30	
15.00	
15.30	
16.00	
16.30	
17.00	
17.30	
18.00	
18.30	
20.00	
20.30	
21.00	
21.30	
22.00	

POWER HOUR

○ _____
○ _____
○ _____
○ _____
○ _____
○ _____
○ _____
○ _____
○ _____
○ _____
○ _____

50-10 METHOD

1. _____ ○
2. _____ ○
3. _____ ○
4. _____ ○
5. _____ ○

NOTES

Scan to meditate:

One moment I want to remember from today is . . .

How can I best stay focused every day?

I have looked after myself today by . . .

LOVE ARISES FROM KNOWING MYSELF DEEPLY

SLEEP TRACKER

MOOD TRACKER

WATER TRACKER

POWER HOUR

5.00
5.30
6.00
6.30
7.00
7.30
8.00
8.30
9.00
9.30
10.00
10.30
11.00
11.30
12.00
12.30
13.00
13.30
14.00
13.30
15.00
15.30
16.00
16.30
17.00
17.30
18.00
18.30
19.00
19.30
20.00
20.30
21.00
21.30
22.00

50-10 METHOD

1.
2.
3.
4.
5.

NOTES

Scan to meditate:

One moment I want to remember from today is . . .

_____

_____

What are three qualities that I love in others?

_____

_____

I have looked after myself today by . . .

_____

_____

I PUT POSITIVE ENERGY INTO EVERYTHING I DO

SATURDAY LIST

1. _____ ◯
2. _____ ◯
3. _____ ◯
4. _____ ◯
5. _____ ◯

SUNDAY LIST

1. _____ ◯
2. _____ ◯
3. _____ ◯
4. _____ ◯
5. _____ ◯

DIGITAL DETOX ◯   SELF-CARE SUNDAY ◯   HAVE FUN ◯

GOALS FOR NEXT WEEK

_____

_____

_____

_____

MIND DUMP

60-MINUTE CALMING CHALLENGE

 Challenge yourself to have a great day. Try to do the following 60-minute calming challenge.

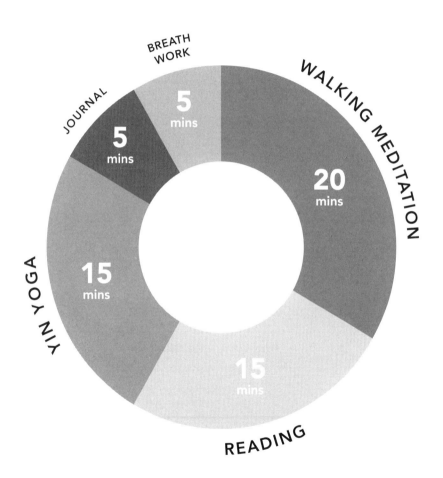

I WILL WAKE UP. SHOW UP. AND NEVER GIVE UP

SLEEP TRACKER	MOOD TRACKER	WATER TRACKER
☽☽☽☽☽☽☽	☺☺☺☺☺	▯▯▯▯▯▯▯

5.00	**POWER HOUR**
5.30	○
6.00	○
6.30	○
7.00	○
7.30	○
8.00	○
8.30	○
9.00	○
9.30	○
10.00	○
10.30	○
11.00	○
11.30	
12.00	
12.30	
13.00	
13.30	
14.00	
13.30	
15.00	
15.30	
16.00	
16.30	**50-10 METHOD**
17.00	1. ○
17.30	2. ○
18.00	3. ○
18.30	4. ○
19.00	5. ○
19.30	
20.00	
20.30	
21.00	
21.30	
22.00	

NOTES

Scan to
meditate:

One moment I want to remember from today is . . .

_____

_____

I like to ground myself by . . .

_____

_____

I have looked after myself today by . . .

_____

_____

REMINDER: I AM RESPONSIBLE FOR WHO I AM

SLEEP TRACKER

☾ ☾ ☾ ☾ ☾ ☾ ☾ ☾

MOOD TRACKER

☺ ☺ ☺ ☺ ☺

WATER TRACKER

▯ ▯ ▯ ▯ ▯ ▯ ▯ ▯

Time	
5.00	
5.30	
6.00	
6.30	
7.00	
7.30	
8.00	
8.30	
9.00	
9.30	
10.00	
10.30	
11.00	
11.30	
12.00	
12.30	
13.00	
13.30	
14.00	
13.30	
15.00	
15.30	
16.00	
16.30	
17.00	
17.30	
18.00	
18.30	
19.00	
19.30	
20.00	
20.30	
21.00	
21.30	
22.00	

POWER HOUR

○ _____
○ _____
○ _____
○ _____
○ _____
○ _____
○ _____
○ _____
○ _____
○ _____
○ _____
○ _____

50-10 METHOD

1. _____ ○
2. _____ ○
3. _____ ○
4. _____ ○
5. _____ ○

NOTES

Scan to meditate:

One moment I want to remember from today is . . .

_____

_____

Something I look forward to every day is:

_____

_____

I have looked after myself today by . . .

_____

_____

EACH DAY IS A CHANCE TO REWRITE MY STORY

SLEEP TRACKER MOOD TRACKER WATER TRACKER

5.00	
5.30	
6.00	
6.30	
7.00	
7.30	
8.00	
8.30	
9.00	
9.30	
10.00	
10.30	
11.00	
11.30	
12.00	
12.30	
13.00	
13.30	
14.00	
13.30	
15.00	
15.30	
16.00	
16.30	
17.00	
17.30	
18.00	
18.30	
19.00	
19.30	
20.00	
20.30	
21.00	
21.30	
22.00	

POWER HOUR

O _____
O _____
O _____
O _____
O _____
O _____
O _____
O _____
O _____
O _____
O _____
O _____

50-10 METHOD

1. _____ O
2. _____ O
3. _____ O
4. _____ O
5. _____ O

NOTES

Scan to
meditate:

One moment I want to remember from today is . . .

This time next month I would like . . .

I have looked after myself today by . . .

THE POWER TO CREATE CHANGE IS IN MY HANDS, SO I CHOOSE TO START TODAY

SLEEP TRACKER

☾ ☾ ☾ ☾ ☾ ☾ ☾ ☾

MOOD TRACKER

☺ ☺ ☺ ☺ ☺

WATER TRACKER

▢ ▢ ▢ ▢ ▢ ▢ ▢ ▢

5.00	
5.30	
6.00	
6.30	
7.00	
7.30	
8.00	
8.30	
9.00	
9.30	
10.00	
10.30	
11.00	
11.30	
12.00	
12.30	
13.00	
13.30	
14.00	
13.30	
15.00	
15.30	
16.00	
16.30	
17.00	
17.30	
18.00	
18.30	
19.00	
19.30	
20.00	
20.30	
21.00	
21.30	
22.00	

POWER HOUR

○ _____
○ _____
○ _____
○ _____
○ _____
○ _____
○ _____
○ _____
○ _____
○ _____
○ _____
○ _____

50-10 METHOD

1. _____ ○
2. _____ ○
3. _____ ○
4. _____ ○
5. _____ ○

NOTES

Scan to
meditate:

One moment I want to remember from today is . . .

How can I stay resilient in tough times?

I have looked after myself today by . . .

I CANNOT MOVE FORWARD WITH THOUGHTS THAT HOLD ME BACK

SLEEP TRACKER

☽ ☽ ☽ ☽ ☽ ☽ ☽ ☽

MOOD TRACKER

☺ ☺ ☺ ☺ ☺

WATER TRACKER

▯ ▯ ▯ ▯ ▯ ▯ ▯ ▯

Time	
5.00	
5.30	
6.00	
6.30	
7.00	
7.30	
8.00	
8.30	
9.00	
9.30	
10.00	
10.30	
11.00	
11.30	
12.00	
12.30	
13.00	
13.30	
14.00	
13.30	
15.00	
15.30	
16.00	
16.30	
17.00	
17.30	
18.00	
18.30	
19.00	
19.30	
20.00	
20.30	
21.00	
21.30	
22.00	

POWER HOUR

○ _____
○ _____
○ _____
○ _____
○ _____
○ _____
○ _____
○ _____
○ _____
○ _____
○ _____
○ _____

50-10 METHOD

1. _____ ○
2. _____ ○
3. _____ ○
4. _____ ○
5. _____ ○

NOTES

Scan to meditate:

One moment I want to remember from today is . . .

_____

_____

What is something that makes me feel alive?

_____

_____

I have looked after myself today by . . .

_____

_____

I AM MINDFUL. TODAY. TOMORROW. ALWAYS

SATURDAY LIST

1. _____ ◯
2. _____ ◯
3. _____ ◯
4. _____ ◯
5. _____ ◯

SUNDAY LIST

1. _____ ◯
2. _____ ◯
3. _____ ◯
4. _____ ◯
5. _____ ◯

DIGITAL DETOX ◯   SELF-CARE SUNDAY ◯   HAVE FUN ◯

GOALS FOR NEXT WEEK

_____

_____

_____

_____

MIND DUMP

SELF-CARE GOALS

Nurture your mind, body and spirit by setting self-care goals for each.
This dedicated list will enhance your well-being.

GOALS: MIND

GOALS: BODY

GOALS: SPIRIT

MY MONTHLY WORK–LIFE BALANCE WHEEL

On a scale of 1 to 10, how am I feeling in the following areas of my work and life? Do not overthink it, just colour it in!

1 ——————————————————————————— **10**

NOT-SO-GREAT   GREAT

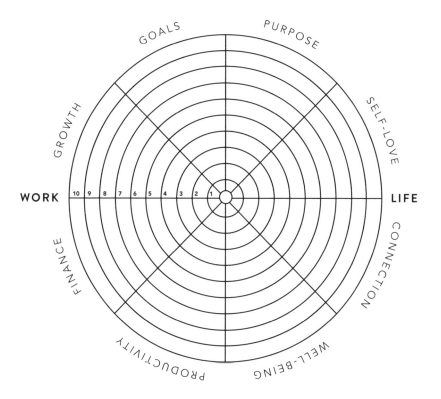

GOALS   PURPOSE

GROWTH   SELF-LOVE

WORK   10 9 8 7 6 5 4 3 2 1   **LIFE**

FINANCE   CONNECTION

PRODUCTIVITY   WELL-BEING

Tip: *Use the space around the wheel to note ways in which you can add more balance to your life.*

MY MONTHLY REVIEW

WHAT WENT WELL THIS MONTH?

DID I STRUGGLE WITH ANYTHING THIS MONTH?

IS THERE ANYTHING I COULD HAVE DONE DIFFERENTLY?

WHAT THREE EMOTIONS RULED MY ENERGY THIS MONTH?

HOW CAN I ADD MORE BALANCE INTO MY LIFE GOING FORWARD?

WHAT IS ONE THING I WANT TO START/DO/ACHIEVE NEXT MONTH?

THE FUTURE IS BUILT ON TODAY. SO LET'S GO!

SLEEP TRACKER

☽ ☽ ☽ ☽ ☽ ☽ ☽ ☽

MOOD TRACKER

☺ ☺ ☺ ☺ ☺

WATER TRACKER

▯ ▯ ▯ ▯ ▯ ▯ ▯ ▯

5.00	
5.30	
6.00	
6.30	
7.00	
7.30	
8.00	
8.30	
9.00	
9.30	
10.00	
10.30	
11.00	
11.30	
12.00	
12.30	
13.00	
13.30	
14.00	
13.30	
15.00	
15.30	
16.00	
16.30	
17.00	
17.30	
18.00	
18.30	
19.00	
19.30	
20.00	
20.30	
21.00	
21.30	
22.00	

POWER HOUR

○ _____
○ _____
○ _____
○ _____
○ _____
○ _____
○ _____
○ _____
○ _____
○ _____
○ _____
○ _____

50-10 METHOD

1. _____ ○
2. _____ ○
3. _____ ○
4. _____ ○
5. _____ ○

NOTES

Scan to meditate:

One moment I want to remember from today is . . .

How do I express my creativity?

I have looked after myself today by . . .

I BELIEVE IN THE MAGIC WITHIN ME

SLEEP TRACKER	MOOD TRACKER	WATER TRACKER

5.00	....
5.30	....
6.00	....
6.30	....
7.00	....
7.30	....
8.00	....
8.30	....
9.00	....
9.30	....
10.00	....
10.30	....
11.00	....
11.30	....
12.00	....
12.30	....
13.00	....
13.30	....
14.00	....
13.30	....
15.00	....
15.30	....
16.00	....
16.30	....
17.00	....
17.30	....
18.00	....
18.30	....
19.00	....
19.30	....
20.00	....
20.30	....
21.00	....
21.30	....
22.00	....

POWER HOUR

○ _____
○ _____
○ _____
○ _____
○ _____
○ _____
○ _____
○ _____
○ _____
○ _____
○ _____
○ _____

50-10 METHOD

1. _____ ○
2. _____ ○
3. _____ ○
4. _____ ○
5. _____ ○

NOTES

Scan to meditate:

One moment I want to remember from today is . . .

What is that one song that puts me in a better mood?

I have looked after myself today by . . .

I CHOOSE TO SHINE BRIGHT. THE WORLD NEEDS MY LIGHT

SLEEP TRACKER
☽ ☽ ☽ ☽ ☽ ☽ ☽ ☽

MOOD TRACKER
☺ ☺ ☺ ☺ ☺

WATER TRACKER
▯ ▯ ▯ ▯ ▯ ▯ ▯ ▯

5.00	
5.30	
6.00	
6.30	
7.00	
7.30	
8.00	
8.30	
9.00	
9.30	
10.00	
10.30	
11.00	
11.30	
12.00	
12.30	
13.00	
13.30	
14.00	
13.30	
15.00	
15.30	
16.00	
16.30	
17.00	
17.30	
18.00	
18.30	
19.00	
19.30	
20.00	
20.30	
21.00	
21.30	
22.00	

POWER HOUR

○ _____
○ _____
○ _____
○ _____
○ _____
○ _____
○ _____
○ _____
○ _____
○ _____
○ _____
○ _____

50-10 METHOD

1. _____ ○
2. _____ ○
3. _____ ○
4. _____ ○
5. _____ ○

NOTES

Scan to meditate:

One moment I want to remember from today is . . .

What recent moment has been pure joy for me?

I have looked after myself today by . . .

THE COMPETITION I FACE IS WITH WHO I WAS YESTERDAY

SLEEP TRACKER

MOOD TRACKER

WATER TRACKER

Time	
5.00	
5.30	
6.00	
6.30	
7.00	
7.30	
8.00	
8.30	
9.00	
9.30	
10.00	
10.30	
11.00	
11.30	
12.00	
12.30	
13.00	
13.30	
14.00	
13.30	
15.00	
15.30	
16.00	
16.30	
17.00	
17.30	
18.00	
18.30	
19.00	
19.30	
20.00	
20.30	
21.00	
21.30	
22.00	

POWER HOUR

○ _____
○ _____
○ _____
○ _____
○ _____
○ _____
○ _____
○ _____
○ _____
○ _____
○ _____
○ _____

50-10 METHOD

1. _____ ○
2. _____ ○
3. _____ ○
4. _____ ○
5. _____ ○

NOTES

Scan to
meditate:

One moment I want to remember from today is . . .

_____

_____

What is something that I can do to manage my days better?

_____

_____

I have looked after myself today by . . .

_____

_____

I USE MY TIME LIKE CURRENCY AND SPEND IT WISELY

SLEEP TRACKER
🌙 🌙 🌙 🌙 🌙 🌙 🌙 🌙

MOOD TRACKER
☺ ☺ ☺ ☺ ☺

WATER TRACKER
▯ ▯ ▯ ▯ ▯ ▯ ▯ ▯

5.00	
5.30	
6.00	
6.30	
7.00	
7.30	
8.00	
8.30	
9.00	
9.30	
10.00	
10.30	
11.00	
11.30	
12.00	
12.30	
13.00	
13.30	
14.00	
13.30	
15.00	
15.30	
16.00	
16.30	
17.00	
17.30	
18.00	
18.30	
19.00	
19.30	
20.00	
20.30	
21.00	
21.30	
22.00	

POWER HOUR

○ _____
○ _____
○ _____
○ _____
○ _____
○ _____
○ _____
○ _____
○ _____
○ _____
○ _____

50-10 METHOD

1. _____ ○
2. _____ ○
3. _____ ○
4. _____ ○
5. _____ ○

NOTES

Scan to
meditate:

One moment I want to remember from today is . . .

What positive changes do I see in myself?

I have looked after myself today by . . .

EVERY SETBACK SETS ME UP FOR A GREATER COMEBACK

SATURDAY LIST

1. _____ ◯
2. _____ ◯
3. _____ ◯
4. _____ ◯
5. _____ ◯

SUNDAY LIST

1. _____ ◯
2. _____ ◯
3. _____ ◯
4. _____ ◯
5. _____ ◯

DIGITAL DETOX ◯   SELF-CARE SUNDAY ◯   HAVE FUN ◯

GOALS FOR NEXT WEEK

_____

_____

_____

_____

MIND DUMP

DOT-TO-DOT

Join the dots to reveal a powerful message just for you.

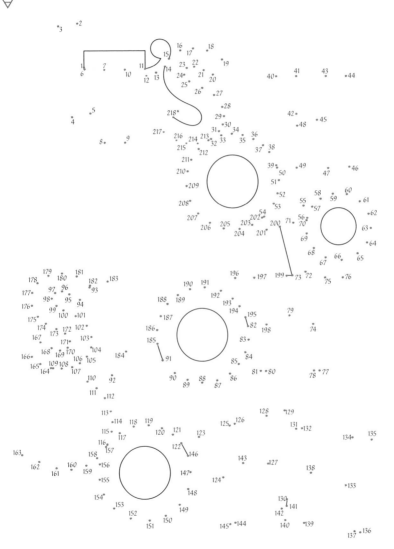

I RADIATE CONFIDENCE, STRENGTH, PERSEVERANCE AND RESILIENCE

SLEEP TRACKER   MOOD TRACKER   WATER TRACKER

5.00
5.30
6.00
6.30
7.00
7.30
8.00
8.30
9.00
9.30
10.00
10.30
11.00
11.30
12.00
12.30
13.00
13.30
14.00
13.30
15.00
15.30
16.00
16.30
17.00
17.30
18.00
18.30
19.00
19.30
20.00
20.30
21.00
21.30
22.00

POWER HOUR

○
○
○
○
○
○
○
○
○
○
○
○

50-10 METHOD

1. _____ ○
2. _____ ○
3. _____ ○
4. _____ ○
5. _____ ○

NOTES

Scan to meditate:

One moment I want to remember from today is . . .

Who is one person I am grateful for?

I have looked after myself today by . . .

REMINDER: I CHOOSE TO LET GO OF ANYTHING THAT HOLDS ME BACK

SLEEP TRACKER   MOOD TRACKER   WATER TRACKER

5.00
5.30
6.00
6.30
7.00
7.30
8.00
8.30
9.00
9.30
10.00
10.30
11.00
11.30
12.00
12.30
13.00
13.30
14.00
13.30
15.00
15.30
16.00
16.30
17.00
17.30
18.00
18.30
19.00
19.30
20.00
20.30
21.00
21.30
22.00

POWER HOUR

50-10 METHOD

1.
2.
3.
4.
5.

NOTES

Scan to
meditate:

One moment I want to remember from today is . . .

_____

_____

How can I keep a positive mindset?

_____

_____

I have looked after myself today by . . .

_____

_____

I AM CLEAR ON MY VISION AND WILL TAKE THE STEPS TO MANIFEST IT

SLEEP TRACKER   MOOD TRACKER   WATER TRACKER

| 5.00 |
| 5.30 |
| 6.00 |
| 6.30 |
| 7.00 |
| 7.30 |
| 8.00 |
| 8.30 |
| 9.00 |
| 9.30 |
| 10.00 |
| 10.30 |
| 11.00 |
| 11.30 |
| 12.00 |
| 12.30 |
| 13.00 |
| 13.30 |
| 14.00 |
| 13.30 |
| 15.00 |
| 15.30 |
| 16.00 |
| 16.30 |
| 17.00 |
| 17.30 |
| 18.00 |
| 18.30 |
| 19.00 |
| 19.30 |
| 20.00 |
| 20.30 |
| 21.00 |
| 21.30 |
| 22.00 |

POWER HOUR

- ○
- ○
- ○
- ○
- ○
- ○
- ○
- ○
- ○
- ○
- ○
- ○
- ○

50-10 METHOD

1. ○
2. ○
3. ○
4. ○
5. ○

NOTES

Scan to meditate:

One moment I want to remember from today is . . .

What positive changes have I made recently?

I have looked after myself today by . . .

ALL THAT POSITIVE ENERGY I GIVE OUT
IS RETURNING TO ME

SLEEP TRACKER   MOOD TRACKER   WATER TRACKER

	POWER HOUR
5.00	○ _____
5.30	○ _____
6.00	○ _____
6.30	○ _____
7.00	○ _____
7.30	○ _____
8.00	○ _____
8.30	○ _____
9.00	○ _____
9.30	○ _____
10.00	○ _____
10.30	○ _____
11.00	○ _____
11.30	
12.00	
12.30	
13.00	
13.30	
14.00	
13.30	
15.00	
15.30	
16.00	

50-10 METHOD

17.00	
17.30	1. _____ ○
18.00	2. _____ ○
18.30	3. _____ ○
19.00	4. _____ ○
19.30	5. _____ ○
20.00	
20.30	
21.00	
21.30	
22.00	

16.30

138 ONE DAY ONE MOMENT

NOTES

Scan to meditate:

One moment I want to remember from today is . . .

How can I practise more mindfulness in my day?

I have looked after myself today by . . .

I WILL BANK ON MYSELF. I WILL STAY AUTHENTIC. I WILL KNOW MY WORTH

SLEEP TRACKER

MOOD TRACKER

WATER TRACKER

		POWER HOUR
5.00		○
5.30		
6.00		○
6.30		
7.00		○
7.30		
8.00		○
8.30		
9.00		○
9.30		
10.00		○
10.30		
11.00		○
11.30		
12.00		○
12.30		
13.00		○
13.30		
14.00		○
13.30		
15.00		○

5.00

5.30

6.00

6.30

7.00

7.30

8.00

8.30

9.00

9.30

10.00

10.30

11.00

11.30

12.00

12.30

13.00

13.30

14.00

13.30

15.00

15.30

16.00

16.30

17.00

17.30

18.00

18.30

19.00

19.30

20.00

20.30

21.00

21.30

22.00

50-10 METHOD

1. _____ ○
2. _____ ○
3. _____ ○
4. _____ ○
5. _____ ○

NOTES

Scan to meditate:

One moment I want to remember from today is . . .

_____

_____

What is one book that changed my life?

_____

_____

I have looked after myself today by . . .

_____

_____

I AM FOCUSED ON PROGRESS, NOT PERFECTION

SATURDAY LIST

1. _____ ○
2. _____ ○
3. _____ ○
4. _____ ○
5. _____ ○

SUNDAY LIST

1. _____ ○
2. _____ ○
3. _____ ○
4. _____ ○
5. _____ ○

DIGITAL DETOX ⬤   SELF-CARE SUNDAY ⬤   HAVE FUN ⬤

GOALS FOR NEXT WEEK

_____
_____
_____
_____

MIND DUMP

WORDSEARCH

Take some time away from your digital device and search for some mindful words to keep your mind topped up with calm.

B	M	E	A	F	P	R	K	V	B	T	U	N	Y	E	X	M	R	K	O
S	K	C	M	S	E	L	F	C	A	R	E	D	B	C	T	O	V	R	J
N	I	O	F	B	J	D	L	O	T	O	L	B	M	E	D	M	B	G	C
R	N	Q	E	P	A	Y	S	E	T	A	T	I	D	E	M	E	K	O	M
X	D	U	B	T	M	E	Q	A	F	B	S	N	O	A	C	N	D	O	B
T	N	E	M	E	V	O	M	N	C	P	F	W	E	N	B	T	V	D	E
V	E	C	A	N	B	E	Y	R	D	K	E	O	U	A	X	F	A	V	R
L	S	E	L	F	L	O	V	E	F	T	L	D	Q	S	P	D	Y	I	L
O	S	B	D	R	X	C	R	E	N	B	D	W	I	E	T	C	N	B	A
M	A	P	F	P	O	W	E	R	I	A	C	O	H	M	A	B	R	E	N
V	U	D	B	A	T	C	S	D	W	L	A	L	E	N	E	Y	C	S	R
E	B	R	O	N	E	K	Z	A	X	B	E	S	A	H	R	A	E	L	U
S	I	A	Z	F	D	S	I	C	E	T	P	B	L	T	B	D	S	T	O
J	Y	S	P	E	L	T	B	J	R	S	F	D	T	M	S	F	O	V	J
W	E	T	B	A	A	O	R	T	B	E	I	P	H	Z	T	Y	P	U	K
K	A	V	O	D	T	M	A	C	W	F	L	O	Y	A	W	P	R	A	E
N	I	G	J	E	I	Y	T	I	V	I	T	I	S	O	P	B	U	C	F
L	S	N	C	A	G	D	S	K	C	N	V	A	X	D	S	E	P	B	M
E	H	A	P	P	I	N	E	S	S	A	K	Q	E	A	C	O	I	C	A
T	F	B	A	R	D	Y	B	A	Z	M	R	A	Y	O	J	N	D	P	J
B	O	P	Z	N	L	E	M	F	C	R	A	Y	B	E	M	V	A	S	D

CRYSTAL	DIGITAL DETOX	KINDNESS	SELF-LOVE	HAPPINESS
GOOD VIBES	SLOW DOWN	POSITIVITY	POWER	HEALTH
GOALS	MOVEMENT	JOURNAL	PURPOSE	MANIFEST
MEDITATE	BELIEVE	MOMENT	JOY	SELF-CARE

I WILL NOT QUIT NOW. MY TIME IS COMING

SLEEP TRACKER   MOOD TRACKER   WATER TRACKER

5.00		POWER HOUR
5.30		
6.00	○	
6.30	○	
7.00	○	
7.30	○	
8.00	○	
8.30	○	
9.00	○	
9.30	○	
10.00	○	
10.30	○	
11.00	○	
11.30	○	
12.00	○	
12.30	○	
13.00	○	
13.30		
14.00		
13.30		
15.00		
15.30		
16.00		
16.30		
17.00		50-10 METHOD
17.30		
18.00		1. ○
18.30		
19.00		2. ○
19.30		3. ○
20.00		
20.30		4. ○
21.00		
21.30		5. ○
22.00		

NOTES

Scan to
meditate:

One moment I want to remember from today is . . .

What positive qualities do my loved ones see in me?

I have looked after myself today by . . .

TUESDAY _____

I WILL NEVER REGRET CHOOSING MYSELF

SLEEP TRACKER   MOOD TRACKER   WATER TRACKER

🌙 🌙 🌙 🌙 🌙 🌙 🌙   ☺ ☺ ☺ ☺ ☺   ⬚⬚⬚⬚⬚⬚⬚⬚

Time		POWER HOUR
5.00		○ _____
5.30		○ _____
6.00		○ _____
6.30		○ _____
7.00		○ _____
7.30		○ _____
8.00		○ _____
8.30		○ _____
9.00		○ _____
9.30		○ _____
10.00		○ _____
10.30		○ _____
11.00		○ _____
11.30		
12.00		
12.30		
13.00		
13.30		
14.00		
13.30		
15.00		
15.30		
16.00		
16.30		
17.00		**50-10 METHOD**
17.30		1. _____ ○
18.00		2. _____ ○
18.30		3. _____ ○
19.00		4. _____ ○
19.30		5. _____ ○
20.00		
20.30		
21.00		
21.30		
22.00		

NOTES

Scan to
meditate:

One moment I want to remember from today is . . .

_____

_____

I am currently trying to manifest . . .

_____

_____

I have looked after myself today by . . .

_____

_____

IF I UPGRADE MY MINDSET, I WILL UPGRADE MY LIFE

SLEEP TRACKER
🌙 🌙 🌙 🌙 🌙 🌙 🌙 🌙

MOOD TRACKER
☺ ☺ ☺ ☺ ☺

WATER TRACKER
▯ ▯ ▯ ▯ ▯ ▯ ▯ ▯

5.00	
5.30	
6.00	
6.30	
7.00	
7.30	
8.00	
8.30	
9.00	
9.30	
10.00	
10.30	
11.00	
11.30	
12.00	
12.30	
13.00	
13.30	
14.00	
13.30	
15.00	
15.30	
16.00	
16.30	
17.00	
17.30	
18.00	
18.30	
19.00	
19.30	
20.00	
20.30	
21.00	
21.30	
22.00	

POWER HOUR

○
○
○
○
○
○
○
○
○
○
○
○

50-10 METHOD

1. _____ ○
2. _____ ○
3. _____ ○
4. _____ ○
5. _____ ○

NOTES

Scan to meditate:

One moment I want to remember from today is . . .

How do I maintain a sense of inner peace?

I have looked after myself today by . . .

I WILL KEEP MY HEAD AND MY VIBES HIGH

SLEEP TRACKER MOOD TRACKER WATER TRACKER

5.00 ....
5.30 ....
6.00 ....
6.30 ....
7.00 ....
7.30 ....
8.00 ....
8.30 ....
9.00 ....
9.30 ....
10.00 ....
10.30 ....
11.00 ....
11.30 ....
12.00 ....
12.30 ....
13.00 ....
13.30 ....
14.00 ....
13.30 ....
15.00 ....
15.30 ....
16.00 ....
16.30 ....
17.00 ....
17.30 ....
18.00 ....
18.30 ....
19.00 ....
19.30 ....
20.00 ....
20.30 ....
21.00 ....
21.30 ....
22.00 ....

POWER HOUR

○ _____
○ _____
○ _____
○ _____
○ _____
○ _____
○ _____
○ _____
○ _____
○ _____
○ _____
○ _____

50-10 METHOD

1. _____ ○
2. _____ ○
3. _____ ○
4. _____ ○
5. _____ ○

NOTES

Scan to meditate:

One moment I want to remember from today is . . .

Something I can do every day and never get bored with is . . .

I have looked after myself today by . . .

TO LIVE FULLY IS TO EMBRACE THE UNKNOWN CONTINUOUSLY

SLEEP TRACKER
🌙 🌙 🌙 🌙 🌙 🌙 🌙 🌙

MOOD TRACKER
☺ ☺ ☺ ☺ ☺

WATER TRACKER
▯ ▯ ▯ ▯ ▯ ▯ ▯ ▯

5.00	**POWER HOUR**
5.30	○ _____
6.00	○ _____
6.30	○ _____
7.00	○ _____
7.30	○ _____
8.00	○ _____
8.30	○ _____
9.00	○ _____
9.30	○ _____
10.00	○ _____
10.30	○ _____
11.00	○ _____
11.30	○ _____
12.00	○ _____
12.30	
13.00	
13.30	
14.00	
13.30	
15.00	
15.30	
16.00	**50-10 METHOD**
16.30	
17.00	1. _____ ○
17.30	2. _____ ○
18.00	3. _____ ○
18.30	4. _____ ○
19.00	5. _____ ○
19.30	
20.00	
20.30	
21.00	
21.30	
22.00	

NOTES

Scan to
meditate:

One moment I want to remember from today is . . .

_____

_____

How do I make more time for activities that I love?

_____

_____

I have looked after myself today by . . .

_____

_____

I AM STRONGER THAN I THINK. I BELIEVE IN MYSELF

SATURDAY LIST

1. _____ ○
2. _____ ○
3. _____ ○
4. _____ ○
5. _____ ○

SUNDAY LIST

1. _____ ○
2. _____ ○
3. _____ ○
4. _____ ○
5. _____ ○

DIGITAL DETOX ●   SELF-CARE SUNDAY ●   HAVE FUN ●

GOALS FOR NEXT WEEK

_____
_____
_____
_____
_____

MIND DUMP

MANIFEST CHALLENGE

Challenge yourself and raise your vibration today. Tick any of the below that you have managed to do recently. One is left blank for you to fill in with something that is personal to you.

REFRAME NEGATIVE
THOUGHTS FOR
THE DAY

RECITE A POSITIVE
AFFIRMATION IN THE
MIRROR

EXPRESS GRATITUDE
THROUGHOUT
THE DAY

CREATE/REFRESH
YOUR VISION
BOARD

DO A MANIFEST MEDITATION

JOURNAL ANY
LIMITING BELIEFS

I RESPOND TO MY EMOTIONS WITH CALM AND CLARITY

SLEEP TRACKER   MOOD TRACKER   WATER TRACKER

5.00	....
5.30	....
6.00	....
6.30	....
7.00	....
7.30	....
8.00	....
8.30	....
9.00	....
9.30	....
10.00	....
10.30	....
11.00	....
11.30	....
12.00	....
12.30	....
13.00	....
13.30	....
14.00	....
13.30	....
15.00	....
15.30	....
16.00	....
16.30	....
17.00	....
17.30	....
18.00	....
18.30	....
19.00	....
19.30	....
20.00	....
20.30	....
21.00	....
21.30	....
22.00	....

POWER HOUR

○ _____
○ _____
○ _____
○ _____
○ _____
○ _____
○ _____
○ _____
○ _____
○ _____
○ _____
○ _____

50-10 METHOD

1. _____ ○
2. _____ ○
3. _____ ○
4. _____ ○
5. _____ ○

NOTES

Scan to
meditate:

One moment I want to remember from today is . . .

How can I better appreciate the present moment?

I have looked after myself today by . . .

REMINDER: I AM NOT AFRAID TO SLOW DOWN

SLEEP TRACKER   MOOD TRACKER   WATER TRACKER

5.00	
5.30	
6.00	
6.30	
7.00	
7.30	
8.00	
8.30	
9.00	
9.30	
10.00	
10.30	
11.00	
11.30	
12.00	
12.30	
13.00	
13.30	
14.00	
13.30	
15.00	
15.30	
16.00	
16.30	
17.00	
17.30	
18.00	
18.30	
19.00	
19.30	
20.00	
20.30	
21.00	
21.30	
22.00	

POWER HOUR

50-10 METHOD

1. _____
2. _____
3. _____
4. _____
5. _____

NOTES

Scan to meditate:

One moment I want to remember from today is . . .

_____

_____

A positive habit that I want to adopt is . . .

_____

_____

I have looked after myself today by . . .

_____

_____

WEDNESDAY

I TAKE INSPIRED ACTION TODAY AND EVERY DAY

SLEEP TRACKER   MOOD TRACKER   WATER TRACKER

5.00
5.30
6.00
6.30
7.00
7.30
8.00
8.30
9.00
9.30
10.00
10.30
11.00
11.30
12.00
12.30
13.00
13.30
14.00
13.30
15.00
15.30
16.00
16.30
17.00
17.30
18.00
18.30
19.00
19.30
20.00
20.30
21.00
21.30
22.00

POWER HOUR

○ _____
○ _____
○ _____
○ _____
○ _____
○ _____
○ _____
○ _____
○ _____
○ _____
○ _____
○ _____

50-10 METHOD

1. _____ ○
2. _____ ○
3. _____ ○
4. _____ ○
5. _____ ○

NOTES

Scan to
meditate:

One moment I want to remember from today is . . .

_____

_____

How do I express gratitude for my health?

_____

_____

I have looked after myself today by . . .

_____

_____

I WILL SLOW DOWN AND RECHARGE AS OFTEN AS I NEED TO

SLEEP TRACKER
🌙 🌙 🌙 🌙 🌙 🌙 🌙 🌙

MOOD TRACKER
☺ ☺ ☺ ☺ ☺

WATER TRACKER
▢ ▢ ▢ ▢ ▢ ▢ ▢ ▢

5.00	
5.30	
6.00	
6.30	
7.00	
7.30	
8.00	
8.30	
9.00	
9.30	
10.00	
10.30	
11.00	
11.30	
12.00	
12.30	
13.00	
13.30	
14.00	
13.30	
15.00	
15.30	
16.00	
16.30	
17.00	
17.30	
18.00	
18.30	
19.00	
19.30	
20.00	
20.30	
21.00	
21.30	
22.00	

POWER HOUR

○ _____
○ _____
○ _____
○ _____
○ _____
○ _____
○ _____
○ _____
○ _____
○ _____
○ _____
○ _____

50-10 METHOD

1. _____ ○
2. _____ ○
3. _____ ○
4. _____ ○
5. _____ ○

NOTES

Scan to
meditate:

One moment I want to remember from today is . . .

How can I celebrate 'me' more?

I have looked after myself today by . . .

IT IS ALL ABOUT MY ACTIONS, NOT MY POSITION

SLEEP TRACKER   MOOD TRACKER   WATER TRACKER

5.00	
5.30	
6.00	
6.30	
7.00	
7.30	
8.00	
8.30	
9.00	
9.30	
10.00	
10.30	
11.00	
11.30	
12.00	
12.30	
13.00	
13.30	
14.00	
13.30	
15.00	
15.30	
16.00	
16.30	
17.00	
17.30	
18.00	
18.30	
19.00	
19.30	
20.00	
20.30	
21.00	
21.30	
22.00	

POWER HOUR

○
○
○
○
○
○
○
○
○
○
○
○

50-10 METHOD

1. _____ ○
2. _____ ○
3. _____ ○
4. _____ ○
5. _____ ○

NOTES

Scan to
meditate:

One moment I want to remember from today is . . .

How have I grown professionally recently?

I have looked after myself today by . . .

EVERY OBSTACLE HAS THE POWER TO TRANSFORM ME

SATURDAY LIST

1. _____ ◯
2. _____ ◯
3. _____ ◯
4. _____ ◯
5. _____ ◯

SUNDAY LIST

1. _____ ◯
2. _____ ◯
3. _____ ◯
4. _____ ◯
5. _____ ◯

DIGITAL DETOX ●   SELF-CARE SUNDAY ●   HAVE FUN ●

GOALS FOR NEXT WEEK

_____

_____

_____

_____

MIND DUMP

BREATH WORK JUST FOR YOU

Discover the benefits of breath work with these two simple techniques: belly breathing and deep breathing. Enhance your well-being and find calmness with these practices.

BELLY BREATHING

TAKE A SLOW, DEEP BREATH IN THROUGH YOUR NOSE, AND FILL YOUR BELLY UP WITH AIR.

HOLD FOR 4 SECONDS.

EXHALE AND RELEASE ALL THE AIR IN YOUR BELLY NICE AND SLOWLY.

REPEAT 5 TIMES.

DEEP BREATHING

TAKE A SLOW, DEEP BREATH IN THROUGH YOUR NOSE FOR 5 SECONDS.

HOLD FOR 5 SECONDS.

EXHALE FOR 5 SECONDS.

REPEAT 5 TIMES.

MY MONTHLY WORK–LIFE BALANCE WHEEL

On a scale of 1 to 10, how am I feeling in the following areas of my work and life? Do not overthink it, just colour it in!

1 ———————————————————————— **10**

NOT-SO-GREAT   GREAT

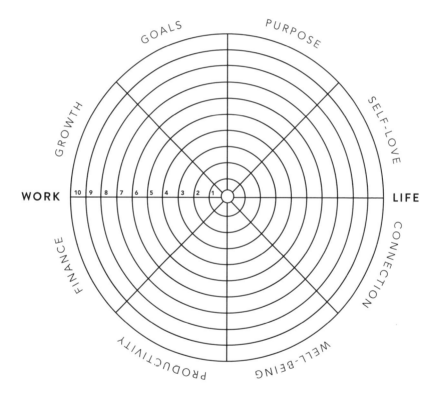

 Tip: Use the space around the wheel to note ways in which you can add more balance to your life.

MY MONTHLY REVIEW

WHAT WENT WELL THIS MONTH?

DID I STRUGGLE WITH ANYTHING THIS MONTH?

IS THERE ANYTHING I COULD HAVE DONE DIFFERENTLY?

WHAT THREE EMOTIONS RULED MY ENERGY THIS MONTH?

HOW CAN I ADD MORE BALANCE INTO MY LIFE GOING FORWARD?

WHAT IS ONE THING I WANT TO START/DO/ACHIEVE NEXT MONTH?

IF I FALL, I KNOW THAT I CAN STILL FLY

SLEEP TRACKER

☽ ☽ ☽ ☽ ☽ ☽ ☽ ☽

MOOD TRACKER

☺ ☺ ☺ ☺ ☺

WATER TRACKER

▢ ▢ ▢ ▢ ▢ ▢ ▢ ▢

Time	
5.00	
5.30	
6.00	
6.30	
7.00	
7.30	
8.00	
8.30	
9.00	
9.30	
10.00	
10.30	
11.00	
11.30	
12.00	
12.30	
13.00	
13.30	
14.00	
13.30	
15.00	
15.30	
16.00	
16.30	
17.00	
17.30	
18.00	
18.30	
19.00	
19.30	
20.00	
20.30	
21.00	
21.30	
22.00	

POWER HOUR

○ _____
○ _____
○ _____
○ _____
○ _____
○ _____
○ _____
○ _____
○ _____
○ _____
○ _____
○ _____

50-10 METHOD

1. _____ ○
2. _____ ○
3. _____ ○
4. _____ ○
5. _____ ○

NOTES

Scan to
meditate:

One moment I want to remember from today is . . .

How can I appreciate the beauty around me?

I have looked after myself today by . . .

NO MATTER HOW BIG OR SMALL, I MAKE THE MOMENTS COUNT

SLEEP TRACKER

☽☽☽☽☽☽☽☽

MOOD TRACKER

☺☺☺☺☺

WATER TRACKER

▢▢▢▢▢▢▢▢

Time	
5.00	
5.30	
6.00	
6.30	
7.00	
7.30	
8.00	
8.30	
9.00	
9.30	
10.00	
10.30	
11.00	
11.30	
12.00	
12.30	
13.00	
13.30	
14.00	
13.30	
15.00	
15.30	
16.00	
16.30	
17.00	
17.30	
18.00	
18.30	
19.00	
19.30	
20.00	
20.30	
21.00	
21.30	
22.00	

POWER HOUR

○ _____
○ _____
○ _____
○ _____
○ _____
○ _____
○ _____
○ _____
○ _____
○ _____
○ _____
○ _____

50-10 METHOD

1. _____ ○
2. _____ ○
3. _____ ○
4. _____ ○
5. _____ ○

NOTES

Scan to meditate:

One moment I want to remember from today is . . .

I am proud of myself because . . .

I have looked after myself today by . . .

I AM NOT WORRIED, MY TIME IS COMING

SLEEP TRACKER

MOOD TRACKER

WATER TRACKER

5.00
5.30
6.00
6.30
7.00
7.30
8.00
8.30
9.00
9.30
10.00
10.30
11.00
11.30
12.00
12.30
13.00
13.30
14.00
13.30
15.00
15.30
16.00
16.30
17.00
17.30
18.00
18.30
19.00
19.30
20.00
20.30
21.00
21.30
22.00

POWER HOUR

- ◯
- ◯
- ◯
- ◯
- ◯
- ◯
- ◯
- ◯
- ◯
- ◯
- ◯
- ◯

50-10 METHOD

1. ◯
2. ◯
3. ◯
4. ◯
5. ◯

NOTES

Scan to meditate:

One moment I want to remember from today is . . .

_____

_____

What in my life has been a blessing in disguise?

_____

_____

I have looked after myself today by . . .

_____

_____

WHERE MY AWARENESS GOES, MY LIFE GROWS

SLEEP TRACKER   MOOD TRACKER   WATER TRACKER

Time	
5.00	
5.30	
6.00	
6.30	
7.00	
7.30	
8.00	
8.30	
9.00	
9.30	
10.00	
10.30	
11.00	
11.30	
12.00	
12.30	
13.00	
13.30	
14.00	
13.30	
15.00	
15.30	
16.00	
16.30	
17.00	
17.30	
18.00	
18.30	
19.00	
19.30	
20.00	
20.30	
21.00	
21.30	
22.00	

POWER HOUR

○ _____
○ _____
○ _____
○ _____
○ _____
○ _____
○ _____
○ _____
○ _____
○ _____
○ _____
○ _____

50-10 METHOD

1. _____ ○
2. _____ ○
3. _____ ○
4. _____ ○
5. _____ ○

NOTES

Scan to meditate:

One moment I want to remember from today is . . .

How can I find more joy in the little things?

I have looked after myself today by . . .

I EMBRACE CHANGE. I AM EVOLVING

SLEEP TRACKER

MOOD TRACKER

WATER TRACKER

| 5.00 |
| 5.30 |
| 6.00 |
| 6.30 |
| 7.00 |
| 7.30 |
| 8.00 |
| 8.30 |
| 9.00 |
| 9.30 |
| 10.00 |
| 10.30 |
| 11.00 |
| 11.30 |
| 12.00 |
| 12.30 |
| 13.00 |
| 13.30 |
| 14.00 |
| 13.30 |
| 15.00 |
| 15.30 |
| 16.00 |
| 16.30 |
| 17.00 |
| 17.30 |
| 18.00 |
| 18.30 |
| 19.00 |
| 19.30 |
| 20.00 |
| 20.30 |
| 21.00 |
| 21.30 |
| 22.00 |

POWER HOUR

50-10 METHOD

1.
2.
3.
4.
5.

NOTES

Scan to meditate:

One moment I want to remember from today is . . .

_____

_____

What empowers me?

_____

_____

I have looked after myself today by . . .

_____

_____

I GIVE LIFE TO WHAT I GIVE ENERGY TO

SATURDAY LIST

1. _____ ○
2. _____ ○
3. _____ ○
4. _____ ○
5. _____ ○

SUNDAY LIST

1. _____ ○
2. _____ ○
3. _____ ○
4. _____ ○
5. _____ ○

DIGITAL DETOX ⬤   SELF-CARE SUNDAY ⬤   HAVE FUN ⬤

GOALS FOR NEXT WEEK

_____
_____
_____
_____
_____

MIND DUMP

MINI VISION BOARD

 Write a personalized mini vision board to visualize your dreams and aspirations. Be as specific as you like and do it with intention.

HEALTH

FINANCE

RELATIONSHIPS

CAREER

TRAVEL

PERSONAL DEVELOPMENT

GROWTH IS HARD, BUT IT IS ALWAYS WORTH IT

SLEEP TRACKER	MOOD TRACKER	WATER TRACKER

5.00 ....
5.30 ....
6.00 ....
6.30 ....
7.00 ....
7.30 ....
8.00 ....
8.30 ....
9.00 ....
9.30 ....
10.00 ....
10.30 ....
11.00 ....
11.30 ....
12.00 ....
12.30 ....
13.00 ....
13.30 ....
14.00 ....
13.30 ....
15.00 ....
15.30 ....
16.00 ....
16.30 ....
17.00 ....
17.30 ....
18.00 ....
18.30 ....
19.00 ....
19.30 ....
20.00 ....
20.30 ....
21.00 ....
21.30 ....
22.00 ....

POWER HOUR

○ _____
○ _____
○ _____
○ _____
○ _____
○ _____
○ _____
○ _____
○ _____
○ _____
○ _____
○ _____

50-10 METHOD

1. _____ ○
2. _____ ○
3. _____ ○
4. _____ ○
5. _____ ○

NOTES

Scan to meditate:

One moment I want to remember from today is . . .

How can I practise more self-compassion?

I have looked after myself today by . . .

REMINDER: I'VE GOT THIS!

SLEEP TRACKER

MOOD TRACKER

WATER TRACKER

5.00	
5.30	
6.00	
6.30	
7.00	
7.30	
8.00	
8.30	
9.00	
9.30	
10.00	
10.30	
11.00	
11.30	
12.00	
12.30	
13.00	
13.30	
14.00	
13.30	
15.00	
15.30	
16.00	
16.30	
17.00	
17.30	
18.00	
18.30	
19.00	
19.30	
20.00	
20.30	
21.00	
21.30	
22.00	

POWER HOUR

50-10 METHOD

1.
2.
3.
4.
5.

NOTES

Scan to meditate:

One moment I want to remember from today is . . .

How can I appreciate life's ups and downs?

I have looked after myself today by . . .

ON DIFFICULT DAYS, I WILL BE EXTRA GENTLE WITH MYSELF

SLEEP TRACKER   MOOD TRACKER   WATER TRACKER

Time	
5.00	
5.30	
6.00	
6.30	
7.00	
7.30	
8.00	
8.30	
9.00	
9.30	
10.00	
10.30	
11.00	
11.30	
12.00	
12.30	
13.00	
13.30	
14.00	
13.30	
15.00	
15.30	
16.00	
16.30	
17.00	
17.30	
18.00	
18.30	
19.00	
19.30	
20.00	
20.30	
21.00	
21.30	
22.00	

POWER HOUR

50-10 METHOD

1.
2.
3.
4.
5.

NOTES

Scan to meditate:

One moment I want to remember from today is . . .

A recent instance where I received encouragement is . . .

I have looked after myself today by . . .

LETTING GO IS THE GIFT I GIVE MYSELF TO MOVE FORWARD

SLEEP TRACKER	MOOD TRACKER	WATER TRACKER
☾ ☾ ☾ ☾ ☾ ☾ ☾ ☾	☺ ☺ ☺ ☺ ☺	⎕ ⎕ ⎕ ⎕ ⎕ ⎕ ⎕ ⎕

5.00	**POWER HOUR**
5.30	○ ....
6.00	○ ....
6.30	○ ....
7.00	○ ....
7.30	○ ....
8.00	○ ....
8.30	○ ....
9.00	○ ....
9.30	○ ....
10.00	○ ....
10.30	○ ....
11.00	○ ....
11.30	○ ....
12.00	○ ....
12.30	
13.00	
13.30	
14.00	
13.30	
15.00	
15.30	**50-10 METHOD**
16.00	
16.30	1. ....○
17.00	2. ....○
17.30	3. ....○
18.00	
18.30	4. ....○
19.00	5. ....○
19.30	
20.00	
20.30	
21.00	
21.30	
22.00	

NOTES

Scan to meditate:

One moment I want to remember from today is . . .

_____

_____

What is something I love about my body?

_____

_____

I have looked after myself today by . . .

_____

_____

EVERYTHING I DO, I DO IT WITH ALL MY HEART

SLEEP TRACKER

MOOD TRACKER

WATER TRACKER

5.00	**POWER HOUR**
5.30	○
6.00	○
6.30	○
7.00	○
7.30	○
8.00	○
8.30	○
9.00	○
9.30	○
10.00	○
10.30	○
11.00	○
11.30	○
12.00	
12.30	
13.00	
13.30	
14.00	
13.30	
15.00	
15.30	
16.00	
16.30	
17.00	**50-10 METHOD**
17.30	
18.00	1. ○
18.30	2. ○
19.00	3. ○
19.30	4. ○
20.00	5. ○
20.30	
21.00	
21.30	
22.00	

NOTES

Scan to meditate:

One moment I want to remember from today is . . .

How can I maintain more balance in my life?

I have looked after myself today by . . .

I MAKE THE PRESENT MOMENT COUNT

SATURDAY LIST

1. _____ ◯
2. _____ ◯
3. _____ ◯
4. _____ ◯
5. _____ ◯

SUNDAY LIST

1. _____ ◯
2. _____ ◯
3. _____ ◯
4. _____ ◯
5. _____ ◯

DIGITAL DETOX ⬤   SELF-CARE SUNDAY ⬤   HAVE FUN ⬤

GOALS FOR NEXT WEEK

_____

_____

_____

_____

MIND DUMP

STAY GROUNDED

Sometimes, we can forget the beauty of being in the 'now'. Doing regular grounding exercises can help you feel calm and help your mind stay more focused on the present rather than looking to the past or future.

5 THINGS I CAN SEE

4 THINGS I CAN FEEL

3 THINGS I CAN HEAR

2 THINGS I CAN SMELL

1 THING I CAN TASTE

 Tip: *Try this exercise whenever you are feeling overwhelmed.*

THE UNIVERSE RESPONDS TO MY ENERGY, SO I VIBE HIGH

SLEEP TRACKER MOOD TRACKER WATER TRACKER

| 5.00 |
| 5.30 |
| 6.00 |
| 6.30 |
| 7.00 |
| 7.30 |
| 8.00 |
| 8.30 |
| 9.00 |
| 9.30 |
| 10.00 |
| 10.30 |
| 11.00 |
| 11.30 |
| 12.00 |
| 12.30 |
| 13.00 |
| 13.30 |
| 14.00 |
| 13.30 |
| 15.00 |
| 15.30 |
| 16.00 |
| 16.30 |
| 17.00 |
| 17.30 |
| 18.00 |
| 18.30 |
| 19.00 |
| 19.30 |
| 20.00 |
| 20.30 |
| 21.00 |
| 21.30 |
| 22.00 |

POWER HOUR

50-10 METHOD

1.
2.
3.
4.
5.

NOTES

Scan to meditate:

One moment I want to remember from today is . . .

_____

_____

How can I stay true to my values?

_____

_____

I have looked after myself today by . . .

_____

_____

I WORK AND LIVE IN ALIGNMENT WITH MY GOALS

SLEEP TRACKER	MOOD TRACKER	WATER TRACKER
☾ ☾ ☾ ☾ ☾ ☾ ☾	☺ ☺ ☺ ☺ ☺	▯▯▯▯▯▯▯▯

5.00 ....
5.30 ....
6.00 ....
6.30 ....
7.00 ....
7.30 ....
8.00 ....
8.30 ....
9.00 ....
9.30 ....
10.00 ....
10.30 ....
11.00 ....
11.30 ....
12.00 ....
12.30 ....
13.00 ....
13.30 ....
14.00 ....
13.30 ....
15.00 ....
15.30 ....
16.00 ....
16.30 ....
17.00 ....
17.30 ....
18.00 ....
18.30 ....
19.00 ....
19.30 ....
20.00 ....
20.30 ....
21.00 ....
21.30 ....
22.00 ....

POWER HOUR

○ _____
○ _____
○ _____
○ _____
○ _____
○ _____
○ _____
○ _____
○ _____
○ _____
○ _____
○ _____

50-10 METHOD

1. _____ ○
2. _____ ○
3. _____ ○
4. _____ ○
5. _____ ○

NOTES

Scan to
meditate:

One moment I want to remember from today is . . .

_____

_____

How can I appreciate myself more?

_____

_____

I have looked after myself today by . . .

_____

_____

I WILL GIVE MYSELF MORE CREDIT. I DESERVE IT

SLEEP TRACKER

🌙 🌙 🌙 🌙 🌙 🌙 🌙 🌙

MOOD TRACKER

☺ ☺ ☺ ☺ ☺

WATER TRACKER

▭ ▭ ▭ ▭ ▭ ▭ ▭ ▭

5.00	
5.30	
6.00	
6.30	
7.00	
7.30	
8.00	
8.30	
9.00	
9.30	
10.00	
10.30	
11.00	
11.30	
12.00	
12.30	
13.00	
13.30	
14.00	
13.30	
15.00	
15.30	
16.00	
16.30	
17.00	
17.30	
18.00	
18.30	
19.00	
19.30	
20.00	
20.30	
21.00	
21.30	
22.00	

POWER HOUR

○ _____
○ _____
○ _____
○ _____
○ _____
○ _____
○ _____
○ _____
○ _____
○ _____
○ _____
○ _____

50-10 METHOD

1. _____ ○
2. _____ ○
3. _____ ○
4. _____ ○
5. _____ ○

NOTES

Scan to
meditate:

One moment I want to remember from today is . . .

_____

_____

What has been the best part of my week so far?

_____

_____

I have looked after myself today by . . .

_____

_____

TOO MANY THOUGHTS LEAVE LITTLE ROOM FOR PEACE

SLEEP TRACKER   MOOD TRACKER   WATER TRACKER

5.00
5.30
6.00
6.30
7.00
7.30
8.00
8.30
9.00
9.30
10.00
10.30
11.00
11.30
12.00
12.30
13.00
13.30
14.00
13.30
15.00
15.30
16.00
16.30
17.00
17.30
18.00
18.30
19.00
19.30
20.00
20.30
21.00
21.30
22.00

POWER HOUR

○
○
○
○
○
○
○
○
○
○
○
○
○

50-10 METHOD

1. ○
2. ○
3. ○
4. ○
5. ○

NOTES

Scan to
meditate:

One moment I want to remember from today is . . .

_____

_____

Is there anything about today I would have done differently?

_____

_____

I have looked after myself today by . . .

_____

_____

I AM TAKING CHARGE OF MY WELL-BEING, PURPOSE AND RELATIONSHIPS

SLEEP TRACKER

🌙 🌙 🌙 🌙 🌙 🌙 🌙

MOOD TRACKER

☺ ☺ ☺ ☺ ☺

WATER TRACKER

▢ ▢ ▢ ▢ ▢ ▢ ▢ ▢

5.00	
5.30	
6.00	
6.30	
7.00	
7.30	
8.00	
8.30	
9.00	
9.30	
10.00	
10.30	
11.00	
11.30	
12.00	
12.30	
13.00	
13.30	
14.00	
13.30	
15.00	
15.30	
16.00	
16.30	
17.00	
17.30	
18.00	
18.30	
19.00	
19.30	
20.00	
20.30	
21.00	
21.30	
22.00	

POWER HOUR

○
○
○
○
○
○
○
○
○
○
○
○

50-10 METHOD

1. _____ ○
2. _____ ○
3. _____ ○
4. _____ ○
5. _____ ○

NOTES

Scan to
meditate:

One moment I want to remember from today is . . .

What recent discovery brought me clarity?

I have looked after myself today by . . .

IT IS OK TO SAY NO TO OTHERS

SATURDAY LIST

1. _____ ○
2. _____ ○
3. _____ ○
4. _____ ○
5. _____ ○

SUNDAY LIST

1. _____ ○
2. _____ ○
3. _____ ○
4. _____ ○
5. _____ ○

DIGITAL DETOX ⬤   SELF-CARE SUNDAY ⬤   HAVE FUN ⬤

GOALS FOR NEXT WEEK

_____

_____

_____

_____

MIND DUMP

COLOURING QUOTE

Colouring is a great way to get into a meditative state by calming the mind and feeling relaxed. Visualize and feel the words below as you colour.

CONSISTENT BEHAVIOURS MATTER

SLEEP TRACKER

MOOD TRACKER

WATER TRACKER

5.00	....
5.30	....
6.00	....
6.30	....
7.00	....
7.30	....
8.00	....
8.30	....
9.00	....
9.30	....
10.00	....
10.30	....
11.00	....
11.30	....
12.00	....
12.30	....
13.00	....
13.30	....
14.00	....
13.30	....
15.00	....
15.30	....
16.00	....
16.30	....
17.00	....
17.30	....
18.00	....
18.30	....
19.00	....
19.30	....
20.00	....
20.30	....
21.00	....
21.30	....
22.00	....

POWER HOUR

O _____
O _____
O _____
O _____
O _____
O _____
O _____
O _____
O _____
O _____
O _____
O _____

50-10 METHOD

1. _____ O
2. _____ O
3. _____ O
4. _____ O
5. _____ O

NOTES

Scan to
meditate:

One moment I want to remember from today is . . .

Something I have always wanted to learn is . . .

I have looked after myself today by . . .

REMINDER: I CAN ALWAYS GET BACK ON TRACK

SLEEP TRACKER

☽ ☽ ☽ ☽ ☽ ☽ ☽ ☽

MOOD TRACKER

☺ ☺ ☺ ☺ ☺

WATER TRACKER

▯ ▯ ▯ ▯ ▯ ▯ ▯ ▯

Time	
5.00	
5.30	
6.00	
6.30	
7.00	
7.30	
8.00	
8.30	
9.00	
9.30	
10.00	
10.30	
11.00	
11.30	
12.00	
12.30	
13.00	
13.30	
14.00	
13.30	
15.00	
15.30	
16.00	
16.30	
17.00	
17.30	
18.00	
18.30	
19.00	
19.30	
20.00	
20.30	
21.00	
21.30	
22.00	

POWER HOUR

○ _____
○ _____
○ _____
○ _____
○ _____
○ _____
○ _____
○ _____
○ _____
○ _____
○ _____

50-10 METHOD

1. _____ ○
2. _____ ○
3. _____ ○
4. _____ ○
5. _____ ○

NOTES

Scan to
meditate:

One moment I want to remember from today is . . .

_____

_____

Who have I learnt the most from and why?

_____

_____

I have looked after myself today by . . .

_____

_____

I AM LOYAL TO MY INTUITION AND CREATE BOUNDARIES

SLEEP TRACKER

🌙🌙🌙🌙🌙🌙🌙🌙

MOOD TRACKER

☺☺☺☺☺

WATER TRACKER

▢▢▢▢▢▢▢▢

5.00	**POWER HOUR**
5.30	○ _____
6.00	
6.30	○ _____
7.00	
7.30	○ _____
8.00	
8.30	○ _____
9.00	
9.30	○ _____
10.00	
10.30	○ _____
11.00	
11.30	○ _____
12.00	
12.30	○ _____
13.00	
13.30	○ _____
14.00	
13.30	○ _____
15.00	
15.30	○ _____
16.00	
16.30	
17.00	**50-10 METHOD**
17.30	
18.00	1. _____ ○
18.30	
19.00	2. _____ ○
19.30	
20.00	3. _____ ○
20.30	
21.00	4. _____ ○
21.30	
22.00	5. _____ ○

NOTES

Scan to meditate:

One moment I want to remember from today is . . .

_____

_____

How can I make the world better?

_____

_____

I have looked after myself today by . . .

_____

_____

I ALLOW MYSELF TO TRY NEW THINGS

SLEEP TRACKER
🌙 🌙 🌙 🌙 🌙 🌙 🌙

MOOD TRACKER
☺ ☺ ☺ ☺ ☺

WATER TRACKER
▢ ▢ ▢ ▢ ▢ ▢ ▢ ▢

5.00	
5.30	
6.00	
6.30	
7.00	
7.30	
8.00	
8.30	
9.00	
9.30	
10.00	
10.30	
11.00	
11.30	
12.00	
12.30	
13.00	
13.30	
14.00	
13.30	
15.00	
15.30	
16.00	
16.30	
17.00	
17.30	
18.00	
18.30	
19.00	
19.30	
20.00	
20.30	
21.00	
21.30	
22.00	

POWER HOUR

○ _____
○ _____
○ _____
○ _____
○ _____
○ _____
○ _____
○ _____
○ _____
○ _____
○ _____
○ _____

50-10 METHOD

1. _____ ○
2. _____ ○
3. _____ ○
4. _____ ○
5. _____ ○

NOTES

Scan to
meditate:

One moment I want to remember from today is . . .

_____

_____

What is an unexpected joy that I have felt recently?

_____

_____

I have looked after myself today by . . .

_____

_____

SELF-LOVE IS ACCEPTING WHO I AM TODAY

SLEEP TRACKER

🌙 🌙 🌙 🌙 🌙 🌙 🌙 🌙

MOOD TRACKER

☺ ☺ ☺ ☺ ☺

WATER TRACKER

▯ ▯ ▯ ▯ ▯ ▯ ▯ ▯

5.00	
5.30	
6.00	
6.30	
7.00	
7.30	
8.00	
8.30	
9.00	
9.30	
10.00	
10.30	
11.00	
11.30	
12.00	
12.30	
13.00	
13.30	
14.00	
13.30	
15.00	
15.30	
16.00	
16.30	
17.00	
17.30	
18.00	
18.30	
19.00	
19.30	
20.00	
20.30	
21.00	
21.30	
22.00	

POWER HOUR

○ _____
○ _____
○ _____
○ _____
○ _____
○ _____
○ _____
○ _____
○ _____
○ _____
○ _____
○ _____

50-10 METHOD

1. _____ ○
2. _____ ○
3. _____ ○
4. _____ ○
5. _____ ○

NOTES

Scan to meditate:

One moment I want to remember from today is . . .

How can I positively embrace change?

I have looked after myself today by . . .

MY REACTION IS MY PAST. MY RESPONSE IS MY FUTURE

SATURDAY LIST

1. _____ ◯
2. _____ ◯
3. _____ ◯
4. _____ ◯
5. _____ ◯

SUNDAY LIST

1. _____ ◯
2. _____ ◯
3. _____ ◯
4. _____ ◯
5. _____ ◯

DIGITAL DETOX ⬤   SELF-CARE SUNDAY ⬤   HAVE FUN ⬤

GOALS FOR NEXT WEEK

_____

_____

_____

_____

_____

MIND DUMP

SELF-BELIEF MAGIC

Believe in the power of yourself and your words. To really feel these positive feelings towards yourself, finish the sentences below.

I AM

I KNOW

I AM PROUD OF

I HAVE

I CHOOSE

I WILL

I CAN

I BELIEVE

MY MONTHLY WORK–LIFE BALANCE WHEEL

 On a scale of 1 to 10, how am I feeling in the following areas of my work and life? Do not overthink it, just colour it in!

1 ———————————————————— **10**

NOT-SO-GREAT   GREAT

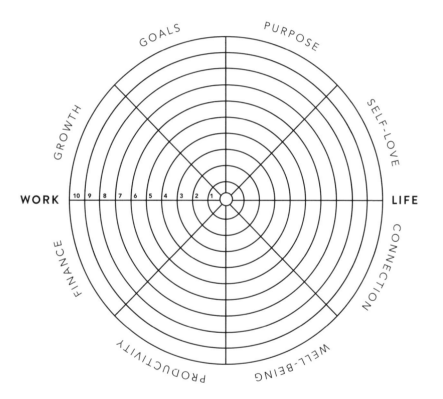

 Tip: *Use the space around the wheel to note ways in which you can add more balance to your life.*

MY MONTHLY REVIEW

WHAT WENT WELL THIS MONTH?

DID I STRUGGLE WITH ANYTHING THIS MONTH?

IS THERE ANYTHING I COULD HAVE DONE DIFFERENTLY?

WHAT THREE EMOTIONS RULED MY ENERGY THIS MONTH?

HOW CAN I ADD MORE BALANCE INTO MY LIFE GOING FORWARD?

WHAT IS ONE THING I WANT TO START/DO/ACHIEVE NEXT MONTH?

I TRUST THAT EVERYTHING IS FALLING INTO PLACE

SLEEP TRACKER

MOOD TRACKER

WATER TRACKER

	POWER HOUR
5.00	○ _____
5.30	○ _____
6.00	○ _____
6.30	○ _____
7.00	○ _____
7.30	○ _____
8.00	○ _____
8.30	○ _____
9.00	○ _____
9.30	○ _____
10.00	○ _____
10.30	○ _____
11.00	
11.30	
12.00	
12.30	
13.00	
13.30	
14.00	
13.30	
15.00	
15.30	
16.00	
16.30	
17.00	**50-10 METHOD**
17.30	
18.00	1. _____ ○
18.30	2. _____ ○
19.00	3. _____ ○
19.30	4. _____ ○
20.00	5. _____ ○
20.30	
21.00	
21.30	
22.00	

NOTES

Scan to
meditate:

One moment I want to remember from today is . . .

_____

_____

What excites me about the future?

_____

_____

I have looked after myself today by . . .

_____

_____

TUESDAY

IT IS OK TO EXPLORE NEW CONNECTIONS THAT FEEL MORE ALIGNED

SLEEP TRACKER   MOOD TRACKER   WATER TRACKER

5.00	POWER HOUR
5.30	O
6.00	O
6.30	O
7.00	O
7.30	O
8.00	O
8.30	O
9.00	O
9.30	O
10.00	O
10.30	O
11.00	O
11.30	O
12.00	
12.30	
13.00	
13.30	
14.00	
13.30	
15.00	
15.30	
16.00	
16.30	
17.00	50-10 METHOD
17.30	
18.00	1. O
18.30	2. O
19.00	3. O
19.30	4. O
20.00	5. O
20.30	
21.00	
21.30	
22.00	

NOTES

Scan to meditate:

One moment I want to remember from today is . . .

What gives me purpose in life?

I have looked after myself today by . . .

THE GROUND WILL HOLD ME. I AM SAFE

SLEEP TRACKER

🌙 🌙 🌙 🌙 🌙 🌙 🌙 🌙

MOOD TRACKER

☺ ☺ ☺ ☺ ☺

WATER TRACKER

▯ ▯ ▯ ▯ ▯ ▯ ▯ ▯

5.00	
5.30	
6.00	
6.30	
7.00	
7.30	
8.00	
8.30	
9.00	
9.30	
10.00	
10.30	
11.00	
11.30	
12.00	
12.30	
13.00	
13.30	
14.00	
13.30	
15.00	
15.30	
16.00	
16.30	
17.00	
17.30	
18.00	
18.30	
19.00	
19.30	
20.00	
20.30	
21.00	
21.30	
22.00	

POWER HOUR

○ _____
○ _____
○ _____
○ _____
○ _____
○ _____
○ _____
○ _____
○ _____
○ _____
○ _____
○ _____

50-10 METHOD

1. _____ ○
2. _____ ○
3. _____ ○
4. _____ ○
5. _____ ○

NOTES

Scan to meditate:

One moment I want to remember from today is . . .

_____

_____

I am naturally good at . . .

_____

_____

I have looked after myself today by . . .

_____

_____

I WILL NOTICE THE SIGNS WHEN I AM ON THE RIGHT PATH

SLEEP TRACKER

🌙 🌙 🌙 🌙 🌙 🌙 🌙 🌙

MOOD TRACKER

☺ ☺ ☺ ☺ ☺

WATER TRACKER

▭ ▭ ▭ ▭ ▭ ▭ ▭ ▭

5.00	
5.30	
6.00	
6.30	
7.00	
7.30	
8.00	
8.30	
9.00	
9.30	
10.00	
10.30	
11.00	
11.30	
12.00	
12.30	
13.00	
13.30	
14.00	
13.30	
15.00	
15.30	
16.00	
16.30	
17.00	
17.30	
18.00	
18.30	
19.00	
19.30	
20.00	
20.30	
21.00	
21.30	
22.00	

POWER HOUR

○ _____
○ _____
○ _____
○ _____
○ _____
○ _____
○ _____
○ _____
○ _____
○ _____
○ _____
○ _____

50-10 METHOD

1. _____ ○
2. _____ ○
3. _____ ○
4. _____ ○
5. _____ ○

NOTES

Scan to
meditate:

One moment I want to remember from today is . . .

What is something I cannot get enough of?

I have looked after myself today by . . .

MY DEEPEST VALUES ARE PRESENT IN EVERY DECISION I MAKE

SLEEP TRACKER   MOOD TRACKER   WATER TRACKER

☽ ☽ ☽ ☽ ☽ ☽ ☽   ☺ ☺ ☺ ☺ ☺   ▯ ▯ ▯ ▯ ▯ ▯ ▯ ▯

Time	
5.00	
5.30	
6.00	
6.30	
7.00	
7.30	
8.00	
8.30	
9.00	
9.30	
10.00	
10.30	
11.00	
11.30	
12.00	
12.30	
13.00	
13.30	
14.00	
13.30	
15.00	
15.30	
16.00	
16.30	
17.00	
17.30	
18.00	
18.30	
19.00	
19.30	
20.00	
20.30	
21.00	
21.30	
22.00	

POWER HOUR

○ _____
○ _____
○ _____
○ _____
○ _____
○ _____
○ _____
○ _____
○ _____
○ _____
○ _____
○ _____

50-10 METHOD

1. _____ ○
2. _____ ○
3. _____ ○
4. _____ ○
5. _____ ○

NOTES

Scan to meditate:

One moment I want to remember from today is . . .

_____

_____

A healthy boundary I have set is . . .

_____

_____

I have looked after myself today by . . .

_____

_____

I AM THE ONE I HAVE BEEN WAITING FOR

SATURDAY LIST

1. _____ ○
2. _____ ○
3. _____ ○
4. _____ ○
5. _____ ○

SUNDAY LIST

1. _____ ○
2. _____ ○
3. _____ ○
4. _____ ○
5. _____ ○

DIGITAL DETOX ○   SELF-CARE SUNDAY ○   HAVE FUN ○

GOALS FOR NEXT WEEK

_____

_____

_____

_____

MIND DUMP

GRATITUDE GARDEN

 Welcome to your very own garden of gratitude. No matter how big or small, take a moment to list everything you are grateful for inside the flowers.

BE REMEMBERED FOR THE WAY YOU MADE PEOPLE FEEL

SLEEP TRACKER

MOOD TRACKER

WATER TRACKER

5.00	
5.30	
6.00	
6.30	
7.00	
7.30	
8.00	
8.30	
9.00	
9.30	
10.00	
10.30	
11.00	
11.30	
12.00	
12.30	
13.00	
13.30	
14.00	
13.30	
15.00	
15.30	
16.00	
16.30	
17.00	
17.30	
18.00	
18.30	
19.00	
19.30	
20.00	
20.30	
21.00	
21.30	
22.00	

POWER HOUR

○ _____
○ _____
○ _____
○ _____
○ _____
○ _____
○ _____
○ _____
○ _____
○ _____
○ _____
○ _____

50-10 METHOD

1. _____ ○
2. _____ ○
3. _____ ○
4. _____ ○
5. _____ ○

NOTES

One moment I want to remember from today is . . .

_____

_____

What is my most treasured memory?

_____

_____

I have looked after myself today by . . .

_____

_____

REMINDER: I FORGIVE THE PAST VERSION OF MYSELF

SLEEP TRACKER	MOOD TRACKER	WATER TRACKER
☾ ☾ ☾ ☾ ☾ ☾ ☾ ☾	☺ ☺ ☺ ☺ ☺	▯ ▯ ▯ ▯ ▯ ▯ ▯ ▯

Time	
5.00	
5.30	
6.00	
6.30	
7.00	
7.30	
8.00	
8.30	
9.00	
9.30	
10.00	
10.30	
11.00	
11.30	
12.00	
12.30	
13.00	
13.30	
14.00	
13.30	
15.00	
15.30	
16.00	
16.30	
17.00	
17.30	
18.00	
18.30	
19.00	
19.30	
20.00	
20.30	
21.00	
21.30	
22.00	

POWER HOUR

○ _____
○ _____
○ _____
○ _____
○ _____
○ _____
○ _____
○ _____
○ _____
○ _____
○ _____
○ _____

50-10 METHOD

1. _____ ○
2. _____ ○
3. _____ ○
4. _____ ○
5. _____ ○

NOTES

Scan to meditate:

One moment I want to remember from today is . . .

What brightened up my day today?

I have looked after myself today by . . .

CHOOSING FAITH OVER FEAR CREATES A PROMISING FUTURE

SLEEP TRACKER MOOD TRACKER WATER TRACKER

			POWER HOUR
5.00		○	
5.30		○	
6.00		○	
6.30		○	
7.00		○	
7.30		○	
8.00		○	
8.30		○	
9.00		○	
9.30		○	
10.00		○	
10.30		○	
11.00		○	
11.30			
12.00			
12.30			
13.00			
13.30			
14.00			
13.30			
15.00			
15.30			
16.00			

50-10 METHOD

1. _____ ○
2. _____ ○
3. _____ ○
4. _____ ○
5. _____ ○

16.30
17.00
17.30
18.00
18.30
19.00
19.30
20.00
20.30
21.00
21.30
22.00

NOTES

Scan to meditate:

One moment I want to remember from today is . . .

A positive thought I am carrying into tomorrow is . . .

I have looked after myself today by . . .

MY LIFE STORY IS ONE OF A KIND

SLEEP TRACKER

MOOD TRACKER

WATER TRACKER

	POWER HOUR
5.00	
5.30	○ _____
6.00	
6.30	○ _____
7.00	
7.30	○ _____
8.00	
8.30	○ _____
9.00	
9.30	○ _____
10.00	
10.30	○ _____
11.00	
11.30	○ _____
12.00	
12.30	○ _____
13.00	
13.30	○ _____
14.00	
13.30	○ _____
15.00	
15.30	○ _____
16.00	
16.30	
17.00	

50-10 METHOD

17.30
18.00   1. _____ ○
18.30
19.00   2. _____ ○
19.30
20.00   3. _____ ○
20.30
21.00   4. _____ ○
21.30
22.00   5. _____ ○

NOTES

Scan to meditate:

One moment I want to remember from today is . . .

Something that made my heart feel light today is . . .

I have looked after myself today by . . .

I PROTECT MY VIBE: I AM KIND AND AVOID GOSSIP AND DRAMA

SLEEP TRACKER	MOOD TRACKER	WATER TRACKER
🌙🌙🌙🌙🌙🌙🌙	☺☺☺☺☺	⬜⬜⬜⬜⬜⬜⬜⬜

5.00	**POWER HOUR**
5.30	○ _____
6.00	○ _____
6.30	○ _____
7.00	○ _____
7.30	○ _____
8.00	○ _____
8.30	○ _____
9.00	○ _____
9.30	○ _____
10.00	○ _____
10.30	○ _____
11.00	○ _____
11.30	○ _____
12.00	
12.30	
13.00	
13.30	
14.00	
13.30	
15.00	
15.30	
16.00	
16.30	
17.00	**50-10 METHOD**
17.30	
18.00	1. _____ ○
18.30	2. _____ ○
19.00	3. _____ ○
19.30	4. _____ ○
20.00	5. _____ ○
20.30	
21.00	
21.30	
22.00	

NOTES

Scan to meditate:

One moment I want to remember from today is . . .

What makes me feel content?

I have looked after myself today by . . .

REMINDER: I WILL ALWAYS AIM TO BE THE BEST VERSION OF MYSELF

SATURDAY LIST

1. _____ ○
2. _____ ○
3. _____ ○
4. _____ ○
5. _____ ○

SUNDAY LIST

1. _____ ○
2. _____ ○
3. _____ ○
4. _____ ○
5. _____ ○

DIGITAL DETOX ⬤   SELF-CARE SUNDAY ⬤   HAVE FUN ⬤

GOALS FOR NEXT WEEK

_____

_____

_____

_____

MIND DUMP

AFFIRM IT

Affirming positive thoughts can have transformative effects. Write out and repeat an affirmation of your choice below.

MY DESIRES WILL DESIRE ME

SLEEP TRACKER
☽ ☽ ☽ ☽ ☽ ☽ ☽ ☽

MOOD TRACKER
☺ ☺ ☺ ☺ ☺

WATER TRACKER
▯ ▯ ▯ ▯ ▯ ▯ ▯ ▯

5.00	
5.30	
6.00	
6.30	
7.00	
7.30	
8.00	
8.30	
9.00	
9.30	
10.00	
10.30	
11.00	
11.30	
12.00	
12.30	
13.00	
13.30	
14.00	
13.30	
15.00	
15.30	
16.00	
16.30	
17.00	
17.30	
18.00	
18.30	
19.00	
19.30	
20.00	
20.30	
21.00	
21.30	
22.00	

POWER HOUR

○ _____
○ _____
○ _____
○ _____
○ _____
○ _____
○ _____
○ _____
○ _____
○ _____
○ _____
○ _____

50-10 METHOD

1. _____ ○
2. _____ ○
3. _____ ○
4. _____ ○
5. _____ ○

NOTES

Scan to meditate:

One moment I want to remember from today is . . .

How can I share joy with others?

I have looked after myself today by . . .

IT IS ALREADY MINE, SO I WILL START BELIEVING IT

SLEEP TRACKER   MOOD TRACKER   WATER TRACKER

5.00	....
5.30	....
6.00	....
6.30	....
7.00	....
7.30	....
8.00	....
8.30	....
9.00	....
9.30	....
10.00	....
10.30	....
11.00	....
11.30	....
12.00	....
12.30	....
13.00	....
13.30	....
14.00	....
13.30	....
15.00	....
15.30	....
16.00	....
16.30	....
17.00	....
17.30	....
18.00	....
18.30	....
19.00	....
19.30	....
20.00	....
20.30	....
21.00	....
21.30	....
22.00	....

POWER HOUR

○ _____
○ _____
○ _____
○ _____
○ _____
○ _____
○ _____
○ _____
○ _____
○ _____
○ _____
○ _____

50-10 METHOD

1. _____ ○
2. _____ ○
3. _____ ○
4. _____ ○
5. _____ ○

NOTES

Scan to
meditate:

One moment I want to remember from today is . . .

How can I make boring tasks more fun?

I have looked after myself today by . . .

DEEP INHALE. DEEP EXHALE. TRANSFORM

SLEEP TRACKER
☾ ☾ ☾ ☾ ☾ ☾ ☾ ☾

MOOD TRACKER
☺ ☺ ☺ ☺ ☺

WATER TRACKER
▯ ▯ ▯ ▯ ▯ ▯ ▯ ▯

Time	
5.00	
5.30	
6.00	
6.30	
7.00	
7.30	
8.00	
8.30	
9.00	
9.30	
10.00	
10.30	
11.00	
11.30	
12.00	
12.30	
13.00	
13.30	
14.00	
13.30	
15.00	
15.30	
16.00	
16.30	
17.00	
17.30	
18.00	
18.30	
19.00	
19.30	
20.00	
20.30	
21.00	
21.30	
22.00	

POWER HOUR

- ○ _____
- ○ _____
- ○ _____
- ○ _____
- ○ _____
- ○ _____
- ○ _____
- ○ _____
- ○ _____
- ○ _____
- ○ _____
- ○ _____

50-10 METHOD

1. _____ ○
2. _____ ○
3. _____ ○
4. _____ ○
5. _____ ○

NOTES

Scan to meditate:

One moment I want to remember from today is . . .

_____

_____

What brings me a sense of fulfillment?

_____

_____

I have looked after myself today by . . .

_____

_____

A NEW RESPONSE TO AN OLD CHALLENGE
SIGNALS GROWTH

SLEEP TRACKER   MOOD TRACKER   WATER TRACKER

5.00	
5.30	**POWER HOUR**
6.00	○
6.30	○
7.00	○
7.30	○
8.00	○
8.30	○
9.00	○
9.30	○
10.00	○
10.30	○
11.00	○
11.30	○
12.00	○
12.30	○
13.00	○
13.30	
14.00	
13.30	
15.00	
15.30	
16.00	
16.30	
17.00	**50-10 METHOD**
17.30	
18.00	1. _____ ○
18.30	2. _____ ○
19.00	3. _____ ○
19.30	4. _____ ○
20.00	5. _____ ○
20.30	
21.00	
21.30	
22.00	

NOTES

Scan to meditate:

One moment I want to remember from today is . . .

How can I improve my quality of sleep?

I have looked after myself today by . . .

I AM NOT FOR EVERYONE, AND EVERYONE IS NOT FOR ME

SLEEP TRACKER   MOOD TRACKER   WATER TRACKER

5.00	POWER HOUR
5.30	
6.00	○
6.30	
7.00	○
7.30	
8.00	○
8.30	
9.00	○
9.30	
10.00	○
10.30	
11.00	○
11.30	
12.00	○
12.30	
13.00	○
13.30	
14.00	○
13.30	
15.00	○
15.30	
16.00	
16.30	
17.00	50-10 METHOD
17.30	
18.00	1. ○
18.30	
19.00	2. ○
19.30	
20.00	3. ○
20.30	
21.00	4. ○
21.30	
22.00	5. ○

NOTES

Scan to
meditate:

One moment I want to remember from today is . . .

_____

_____

How can I bring more enthusiasm to a task?

_____

_____

I have looked after myself today by . . .

_____

_____

I LIVE IN THE MOMENT, NOT FOR THE MOMENT

SATURDAY LIST

1. _____ ○
2. _____ ○
3. _____ ○
4. _____ ○
5. _____ ○

SUNDAY LIST

1. _____ ○
2. _____ ○
3. _____ ○
4. _____ ○
5. _____ ○

DIGITAL DETOX ●   SELF-CARE SUNDAY ●   HAVE FUN ●

GOALS FOR NEXT WEEK

_____

_____

_____

_____

MIND DUMP

WHAT'S IN YOUR CONTROL?

Have a think about what you can control in your life and what you cannot. Channel your energy into what is within your power and practise acceptance for the rest. Write what is in your control inside the circle below, and list the things you do not have control over outside of the circle.

IT IS NOT TOO LATE TO CREATE A BEAUTIFUL AND FULFILLING LIFE

SLEEP TRACKER ☽☽☽☽☽☽☽☽

MOOD TRACKER ☺☺☺☺☺

WATER TRACKER ▯▯▯▯▯▯▯▯

5.00	
5.30	
6.00	
6.30	
7.00	
7.30	
8.00	
8.30	
9.00	
9.30	
10.00	
10.30	
11.00	
11.30	
12.00	
12.30	
13.00	
13.30	
14.00	
13.30	
15.00	
15.30	
16.00	
16.30	
17.00	
17.30	
18.00	
18.30	
19.00	
19.30	
20.00	
20.30	
21.00	
21.30	
22.00	

POWER HOUR

○
○
○
○
○
○
○
○
○
○
○
○

50-10 METHOD

1. ○
2. ○
3. ○
4. ○
5. ○

NOTES

Scan to
meditate:

One moment I want to remember from today is . . .

How can I uplift my spirit more?

I have looked after myself today by . . .

REMINDER: NOBODY ELSE'S OPINION OF ME MATTERS

SLEEP TRACKER

🌙 🌙 🌙 🌙 🌙 🌙 🌙 🌙

MOOD TRACKER

☺ ☺ ☺ ☺ ☺

WATER TRACKER

▭ ▭ ▭ ▭ ▭ ▭ ▭ ▭

5.00	
5.30	
6.00	
6.30	
7.00	
7.30	
8.00	
8.30	
9.00	
9.30	
10.00	
10.30	
11.00	
11.30	
12.00	
12.30	
13.00	
13.30	
14.00	
13.30	
15.00	
15.30	
16.00	
16.30	
17.00	
17.30	
18.00	
18.30	
19.00	
19.30	
20.00	
20.30	
21.00	
21.30	
22.00	

POWER HOUR

○ _____
○ _____
○ _____
○ _____
○ _____
○ _____
○ _____
○ _____
○ _____
○ _____
○ _____
○ _____

50-10 METHOD

1. _____ ○
2. _____ ○
3. _____ ○
4. _____ ○
5. _____ ○

NOTES

Scan to meditate:

One moment I want to remember from today is . . .

How can I bring more joy into my career?

I have looked after myself today by . . .

I AM CAPABLE OF OVERCOMING HARD TIMES

SLEEP TRACKER   MOOD TRACKER   WATER TRACKER

Time	
5.00	
5.30	
6.00	
6.30	
7.00	
7.30	
8.00	
8.30	
9.00	
9.30	
10.00	
10.30	
11.00	
11.30	
12.00	
12.30	
13.00	
13.30	
14.00	
13.30	
15.00	
15.30	
16.00	
16.30	
17.00	
17.30	
18.00	
18.30	
19.00	
19.30	
20.00	
20.30	
21.00	
21.30	
22.00	

POWER HOUR

50-10 METHOD

1.
2.
3.
4.
5.

NOTES

Scan to meditate:

One moment I want to remember from today is . . .

_____

_____

How can I turn a challenge into a learning opportunity?

_____

_____

I have looked after myself today by . . .

_____

_____

THE UNIVERSE RESPONDS TO MY
ENERGETIC FREQUENCY

SLEEP TRACKER   MOOD TRACKER   WATER TRACKER

5.00		POWER HOUR
5.30		○
6.00		○
6.30		○
7.00		○
7.30		○
8.00		○
8.30		○
9.00		○
9.30		○
10.00		○
10.30		○
11.00		○
11.30		○
12.00		
12.30		
13.00		
13.30		
14.00		
13.30		
15.00		

15.30
16.00
16.30
17.00	50-10 METHOD
17.30	
18.00	1. ○
18.30	2. ○
19.00	3. ○
19.30	4. ○
20.00	5. ○
20.30
21.00
21.30
22.00

NOTES

Scan to meditate:

One moment I want to remember from today is . . .

What do I value the most in relationships?

I have looked after myself today by . . .

FRIDAY _____

I WILL LET GO OF WHAT DOES NOT
BELONG IN MY LIFE

SLEEP TRACKER   MOOD TRACKER   WATER TRACKER

🌙 🌙 🌙 🌙 🌙 🌙 🌙 🌙   ☺ ☺ ☺ ☺ ☺

	POWER HOUR
5.00	○
5.30	
6.00	○
6.30	
7.00	○
7.30	
8.00	○
8.30	
9.00	○
9.30	
10.00	○
10.30	
11.00	○
11.30	
12.00	○
12.30	
13.00	○
13.30	
14.00	○
13.30	
15.00	○

5.00
5.30
6.00
6.30
7.00
7.30
8.00
8.30
9.00
9.30
10.00
10.30
11.00
11.30
12.00
12.30
13.00
13.30
14.00
13.30
15.00
15.30
16.00
16.30
17.00
17.30
18.00
18.30
19.00
19.30
20.00
20.30
21.00
21.30
22.00

50-10 METHOD

1. _____ ○
2. _____ ○
3. _____ ○
4. _____ ○
5. _____ ○

NOTES

Scan to meditate:

One moment I want to remember from today is . . .

This is how I would describe my day in one positive word:

I have looked after myself today by . . .

I REMEMBER WHO I AM AND WHAT I STAND FOR

SATURDAY LIST

1. _____ ○
2. _____ ○
3. _____ ○
4. _____ ○
5. _____ ○

SUNDAY LIST

1. _____ ○
2. _____ ○
3. _____ ○
4. _____ ○
5. _____ ○

DIGITAL DETOX ●   SELF-CARE SUNDAY ●   HAVE FUN ●

GOALS FOR NEXT WEEK

_____

_____

_____

_____

MIND DUMP

I AM AWESOME

You are awesome and we want you to know that! Write down all the reasons why you are awesome below.

I AM AWESOME BECAUSE

_____

_____

I AM AWESOME BECAUSE

_____

_____

I AM AWESOME BECAUSE

_____

_____

I AM AWESOME BECAUSE

_____

_____

I AM AWESOME BECAUSE

_____

_____

I AM AWESOME BECAUSE

_____

_____

MY MONTHLY WORK–LIFE BALANCE WHEEL

 On a scale of 1 to 10, how am I feeling in the following areas of my work and life? Do not overthink it, just colour it in!

1 ———————————————————— **10**

NOT-SO-GREAT   GREAT

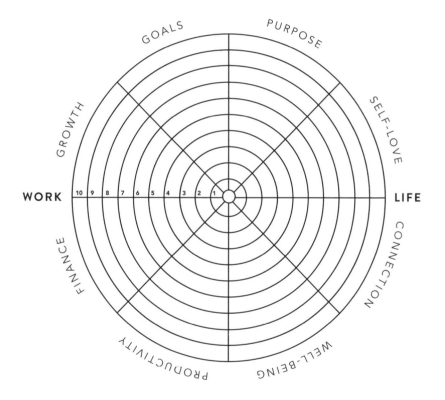

 Tip: *Use the space around the wheel to note ways in which you can add more balance to your life.*

MY MONTHLY REVIEW

WHAT WENT WELL THIS MONTH?

DID I STRUGGLE WITH ANYTHING THIS MONTH?

IS THERE ANYTHING I COULD HAVE DONE DIFFERENTLY?

WHAT THREE EMOTIONS RULED MY ENERGY THIS MONTH?

HOW CAN I ADD MORE BALANCE INTO MY LIFE GOING FORWARD?

WHAT IS ONE THING I WANT TO START/DO/ACHIEVE NEXT MONTH?

I LET IT COME. I LET IT GO. I LET IT FLOW

SLEEP TRACKER   MOOD TRACKER   WATER TRACKER

5.00
5.30
6.00
6.30
7.00
7.30
8.00
8.30
9.00
9.30
10.00
10.30
11.00
11.30
12.00
12.30
13.00
13.30
14.00
13.30
15.00
15.30
16.00
16.30
17.00
17.30
18.00
18.30
19.00
19.30
20.00
20.30
21.00
21.30
22.00

POWER HOUR

50-10 METHOD

1.
2.
3.
4.
5.

NOTES

Scan to meditate:

One moment I want to remember from today is . . .

Tomorrow I will . . .

I have looked after myself today by . . .

TRUE SUCCESS IS A FEELING I EARN FOR MYSELF

SLEEP TRACKER   MOOD TRACKER   WATER TRACKER

5.00	
5.30	
6.00	POWER HOUR
6.30	

5.00 ....
5.30 ....
6.00 ....
6.30 ....
7.00 ....
7.30 ....
8.00 ....
8.30 ....
9.00 ....
9.30 ....
10.00 ....
10.30 ....
11.00 ....
11.30 ....
12.00 ....
12.30 ....
13.00 ....
13.30 ....
14.00 ....
13.30 ....
15.00 ....
15.30 ....
16.00 ....
16.30 ....
17.00 ....
17.30 ....
18.00 ....
18.30 ....
19.00 ....
19.30 ....
20.00 ....
20.30 ....
21.00 ....
21.30 ....
22.00 ....

POWER HOUR

○ _____
○ _____
○ _____
○ _____
○ _____
○ _____
○ _____
○ _____
○ _____
○ _____
○ _____
○ _____

50-10 METHOD

1. _____ ○
2. _____ ○
3. _____ ○
4. _____ ○
5. _____ ○

NOTES

Scan to meditate:

One moment I want to remember from today is . . .

How can I give back more?

I have looked after myself today by . . .

I AM THE CEO OF MY OWN LIFE

SLEEP TRACKER

🌙 🌙 🌙 🌙 🌙 🌙 🌙 🌙

MOOD TRACKER

☺ ☺ ☺ ☺ ☺

WATER TRACKER

⬜ ⬜ ⬜ ⬜ ⬜ ⬜ ⬜ ⬜

Time	
5.00	
5.30	
6.00	
6.30	
7.00	
7.30	
8.00	
8.30	
9.00	
9.30	
10.00	
10.30	
11.00	
11.30	
12.00	
12.30	
13.00	
13.30	
14.00	
13.30	
15.00	
15.30	
16.00	
16.30	
17.00	
17.30	
18.00	
18.30	
19.00	
19.30	
20.00	
20.30	
21.00	
21.30	
22.00	

POWER HOUR

○ _____
○ _____
○ _____
○ _____
○ _____
○ _____
○ _____
○ _____
○ _____
○ _____
○ _____
○ _____

50-10 METHOD

1. _____ ○
2. _____ ○
3. _____ ○
4. _____ ○
5. _____ ○

NOTES

Scan to
meditate:

One moment I want to remember from today is . . .

_____

_____

Something I can not live without is . . .

_____

_____

I have looked after myself today by . . .

_____

_____

INSTEAD OF FOCUSING ON LIMITS, I CHOOSE TO BE LIMITLESS

SLEEP TRACKER   MOOD TRACKER   WATER TRACKER

5.00	....
5.30	....
6.00	....
6.30	....
7.00	....
7.30	....
8.00	....
8.30	....
9.00	....
9.30	....
10.00	....
10.30	....
11.00	....
11.30	....
12.00	....
12.30	....
13.00	....
13.30	....
14.00	....
13.30	....
15.00	....
15.30	....
16.00	....
16.30	....
17.00	....
17.30	....
18.00	....
18.30	....
19.00	....
19.30	....
20.00	....
20.30	....
21.00	....
21.30	....
22.00	....

POWER HOUR

○ _____
○ _____
○ _____
○ _____
○ _____
○ _____
○ _____
○ _____
○ _____
○ _____
○ _____
○ _____

50-10 METHOD

1. _____ ○
2. _____ ○
3. _____ ○
4. _____ ○
5. _____ ○

NOTES

Scan to meditate:

One moment I want to remember from today is . . .

_____

_____

My favourite positive habit of mine is . . .

_____

_____

I have looked after myself today by . . .

_____

_____

REAL LOVE IS FULL OF ACCEPTANCE, NOT EXPECTATION

SLEEP TRACKER

🌙 🌙 🌙 🌙 🌙 🌙 🌙 🌙

MOOD TRACKER

☺ ☺ ☺ ☺ ☺

WATER TRACKER

▯ ▯ ▯ ▯ ▯ ▯ ▯ ▯

5.00	
5.30	
6.00	
6.30	
7.00	
7.30	
8.00	
8.30	
9.00	
9.30	
10.00	
10.30	
11.00	
11.30	
12.00	
12.30	
13.00	
13.30	
14.00	
13.30	
15.00	
15.30	
16.00	
16.30	
17.00	
17.30	
18.00	
18.30	
19.00	
19.30	
20.00	
20.30	
21.00	
21.30	
22.00	

POWER HOUR

○ _____
○ _____
○ _____
○ _____
○ _____
○ _____
○ _____
○ _____
○ _____
○ _____
○ _____
○ _____

50-10 METHOD

1. _____ ○
2. _____ ○
3. _____ ○
4. _____ ○
5. _____ ○

NOTES

Scan to
meditate:

One moment I want to remember from today is . . .

Something or someone that gives me hope is . . .

I have looked after myself today by . . .

DEEP BREATH IN, AND I LET IT GO, READY FOR THE DAY

SATURDAY LIST

1. _____ ○
2. _____ ○
3. _____ ○
4. _____ ○
5. _____ ○

SUNDAY LIST

1. _____ ○
2. _____ ○
3. _____ ○
4. _____ ○
5. _____ ○

DIGITAL DETOX ●   SELF-CARE SUNDAY ●   HAVE FUN ●

GOALS FOR NEXT WEEK

_____

_____

_____

_____

MIND DUMP

COLOUR AND CALM

 Engage in the gentle rhythm of colouring and quiet the mind, soothe the nerves and promote relaxation. Colour the image below and stay calm.

I AM SOMEONE WHO MAKES ME HAPPY

SLEEP TRACKER   MOOD TRACKER   WATER TRACKER

5.00	POWER HOUR
5.30	
6.00	○ _____
6.30	○ _____
7.00	○ _____
7.30	○ _____
8.00	○ _____
8.30	○ _____
9.00	○ _____
9.30	○ _____
10.00	○ _____
10.30	○ _____
11.00	○ _____
11.30	○ _____
12.00	
12.30	
13.00	
13.30	
14.00	
13.30	
15.00	
15.30	
16.00	
16.30	
17.00	50-10 METHOD
17.30	
18.00	1. _____ ○
18.30	2. _____ ○
19.00	3. _____ ○
19.30	4. _____ ○
20.00	5. _____ ○
20.30	
21.00	
21.30	
22.00	

NOTES

Scan to
meditate:

One moment I want to remember from today is . . .

Three uplifting words that describe me are . . .

I have looked after myself today by . . .

EVERYTHING I WANT WILL COME WHEN THE TIME IS RIGHT

SLEEP TRACKER ☽☽☽☽☽☽☽☽

MOOD TRACKER ☺☺☺☺☺

WATER TRACKER 🥛🥛🥛🥛🥛🥛🥛🥛

Time	
5.00	
5.30	
6.00	
6.30	
7.00	
7.30	
8.00	
8.30	
9.00	
9.30	
10.00	
10.30	
11.00	
11.30	
12.00	
12.30	
13.00	
13.30	
14.00	
13.30	
15.00	
15.30	
16.00	
16.30	
17.00	
17.30	
18.00	
18.30	
19.00	
19.30	
20.00	
20.30	
21.00	
21.30	
22.00	

POWER HOUR

○ _____
○ _____
○ _____
○ _____
○ _____
○ _____
○ _____
○ _____
○ _____
○ _____
○ _____
○ _____

50-10 METHOD

1. _____ ○
2. _____ ○
3. _____ ○
4. _____ ○
5. _____ ○

NOTES

Scan to
meditate:

One moment I want to remember from today is . . .

_____

_____

I feel comfortable when . . .

_____

_____

I have looked after myself today by . . .

_____

_____

SOME DAYS IT RAINS, BUT LIKE THE SUN, I WILL KEEP SHOWING UP

SLEEP TRACKER   MOOD TRACKER   WATER TRACKER

5.00		POWER HOUR
5.30		○ _____
6.00		○ _____
6.30		○ _____
7.00		○ _____
7.30		○ _____
8.00		○ _____
8.30		○ _____
9.00		○ _____
9.30		○ _____
10.00		○ _____
10.30		○ _____
11.00		○ _____
11.30		○ _____
12.00		
12.30		
13.00		
13.30		
14.00		
13.30		
15.00		
15.30		
16.00		
16.30		
17.00		50-10 METHOD
17.30		
18.00		1. _____ ○
18.30		2. _____ ○
19.00		3. _____ ○
19.30		4. _____ ○
20.00		5. _____ ○
20.30		
21.00		
21.30		
22.00		

NOTES

Scan to
meditate:

One moment I want to remember from today is . . .

I feel proud that I have learnt to . . .

I have looked after myself today by . . .

I CAN SURVIVE EVERY HARD DAY

SLEEP TRACKER

☽ ☽ ☽ ☽ ☽ ☽ ☽ ☽

MOOD TRACKER

☺ ☺ ☺ ☺ ☺

WATER TRACKER

▯ ▯ ▯ ▯ ▯ ▯ ▯ ▯

5.00	**POWER HOUR**
5.30	○ _____
6.00	
6.30	○ _____
7.00	
7.30	○ _____
8.00	
8.30	○ _____
9.00	
9.30	○ _____
10.00	
10.30	○ _____
11.00	
11.30	○ _____
12.00	
12.30	○ _____
13.00	
13.30	○ _____
14.00	
13.30	○ _____
15.00	○ _____

5.00
5.30
6.00
6.30
7.00
7.30
8.00
8.30
9.00
9.30
10.00
10.30
11.00
11.30
12.00
12.30
13.00
13.30
14.00
13.30
15.00
15.30
16.00
16.30
17.00
17.30
18.00
18.30
19.00
19.30
20.00
20.30
21.00
21.30
22.00

50-10 METHOD

1. _____ ○
2. _____ ○
3. _____ ○
4. _____ ○
5. _____ ○

NOTES

Scan to meditate:

One moment I want to remember from today is . . .

_____

_____

The person that I last had an inspiring conversation with is . . .

_____

_____

I have looked after myself today by . . .

_____

_____

REJECTIONS REDIRECT ME TO BETTER THINGS

SLEEP TRACKER   MOOD TRACKER   WATER TRACKER

5.00	
5.30	**POWER HOUR**
6.00	○
6.30	○
7.00	○
7.30	○
8.00	○
8.30	○
9.00	○
9.30	○
10.00	○
10.30	○
11.00	○
11.30	○
12.00	○
12.30	○
13.00	○
13.30	
14.00	
13.30	
15.00	
15.30	
16.00	
16.30	
17.00	**50-10 METHOD**
17.30	
18.00	1. ○
18.30	
19.00	2. ○
19.30	3. ○
20.00	
20.30	4. ○
21.00	
21.30	5. ○
22.00	

NOTES

Scan to
meditate:

One moment I want to remember from today is . . .

I feel most like myself when . . .

I have looked after myself today by . . .

MY VISION IS MY MISSION. I AM GROUNDED IN IT

SATURDAY LIST

1. _____ ○
2. _____ ○
3. _____ ○
4. _____ ○
5. _____ ○

SUNDAY LIST

1. _____ ○
2. _____ ○
3. _____ ○
4. _____ ○
5. _____ ○

DIGITAL DETOX ●   SELF-CARE SUNDAY ●   HAVE FUN ●

GOALS FOR NEXT WEEK

_____
_____
_____
_____
_____

MIND DUMP

WORD SCRAMBLE

Unscramble to unveil a message just for you.

——— ——— ———
CEAEP DNA LCAM

—— — ——— —— ——
AER A TPAR FO YM

——— ——— ———
VYEER ADY FEIL

I THINK IT. I FEEL IT. I SPEAK IT. I ACTION IT.
I MANIFEST IT

SLEEP TRACKER   MOOD TRACKER   WATER TRACKER

5.00
5.30
6.00
6.30
7.00
7.30
8.00
8.30
9.00
9.30
10.00
10.30
11.00
11.30
12.00
12.30
13.00
13.30
14.00
13.30
15.00
15.30
16.00
16.30
17.00
17.30
18.00
18.30
19.00
19.30
20.00
20.30
21.00
21.30
22.00

POWER HOUR

50-10 METHOD

1.
2.
3.
4.
5.

NOTES

Scan to meditate:

One moment I want to remember from today is . . .

Something that I really admire is . . .

I have looked after myself today by . . .

LIFE HAPPENS FOR ME, NOT TO ME

SLEEP TRACKER

MOOD TRACKER

WATER TRACKER

Time	
5.00	
5.30	
6.00	
6.30	
7.00	
7.30	
8.00	
8.30	
9.00	
9.30	
10.00	
10.30	
11.00	
11.30	
12.00	
12.30	
13.00	
13.30	
14.00	
13.30	
15.00	
15.30	
16.00	
16.30	
17.00	
17.30	
18.00	
18.30	
19.00	
19.30	
20.00	
20.30	
21.00	
21.30	
22.00	

POWER HOUR

- ⭘
- ⭘
- ⭘
- ⭘
- ⭘
- ⭘
- ⭘
- ⭘
- ⭘
- ⭘
- ⭘
- ⭘

50-10 METHOD

1. _____ ⭘
2. _____ ⭘
3. _____ ⭘
4. _____ ⭘
5. _____ ⭘

NOTES

Scan to meditate:

One moment I want to remember from today is . . .

What is something that I love about my mind?

I have looked after myself today by . . .

I DO NOT NEED TO BE LOUD TO BE HEARD

SLEEP TRACKER   MOOD TRACKER   WATER TRACKER

5.00	....
5.30	....
6.00	....
6.30	....
7.00	....
7.30	....
8.00	....
8.30	....
9.00	....
9.30	....
10.00	....
10.30	....
11.00	....
11.30	....
12.00	....
12.30	....
13.00	....
13.30	....
14.00	....
13.30	....
15.00	....
15.30	....
16.00	....
16.30	....
17.00	....
17.30	....
18.00	....
18.30	....
19.00	....
19.30	....
20.00	....
20.30	....
21.00	....
21.30	....
22.00	....

POWER HOUR

○ _____
○ _____
○ _____
○ _____
○ _____
○ _____
○ _____
○ _____
○ _____
○ _____
○ _____

50-10 METHOD

1. _____ ○
2. _____ ○
3. _____ ○
4. _____ ○
5. _____ ○

NOTES

Scan to meditate:

One moment I want to remember from today is . . .

_____

_____

I feel like I am in my element when . . .

_____

_____

I have looked after myself today by . . .

_____

_____

HAPPINESS IS RIGHT HERE, RIGHT NOW

SLEEP TRACKER MOOD TRACKER WATER TRACKER

5.00	
5.30	
6.00	
6.30	
7.00	
7.30	
8.00	
8.30	
9.00	
9.30	
10.00	
10.30	
11.00	
11.30	
12.00	
12.30	
13.00	
13.30	
14.00	
13.30	
15.00	
15.30	
16.00	
16.30	
17.00	
17.30	
18.00	
18.30	
19.00	
19.30	
20.00	
20.30	
21.00	
21.30	
22.00	

POWER HOUR

50-10 METHOD

1.
2.
3.
4.
5.

NOTES

Scan to meditate:

One moment I want to remember from today is . . .

My last selfless act was . . .

I have looked after myself today by . . .

A SMALL ACT OF KINDNESS CAN BRIGHTEN SOMEONE'S ENTIRE DAY

SLEEP TRACKER   MOOD TRACKER   WATER TRACKER

🌙 🌙 🌙 🌙 🌙 🌙 🌙 🌙   ☺ ☺ ☺ ☺ ☺   ☐ ☐ ☐ ☐ ☐ ☐ ☐ ☐

5.00	**POWER HOUR**
5.30	
6.00	○ _____
6.30	
7.00	○ _____
7.30	
8.00	○ _____
8.30	
9.00	○ _____
9.30	
10.00	○ _____
10.30	
11.00	○ _____
11.30	
12.00	○ _____
12.30	
13.00	○ _____
13.30	
14.00	○ _____
13.30	
15.00	○ _____
15.30	
16.00	
16.30	
17.00	**50-10 METHOD**
17.30	
18.00	1. _____ ○
18.30	
19.00	2. _____ ○
19.30	
20.00	3. _____ ○
20.30	
21.00	4. _____ ○
21.30	
22.00	5. _____ ○

NOTES

Scan to meditate:

One moment I want to remember from today is . . .

How do I like to raise my vibrations?

I have looked after myself today by . . .

I CHOOSE TO SURROUND MYSELF WITH HIGH-VIBING PEOPLE

SATURDAY LIST

1. _____ ○
2. _____ ○
3. _____ ○
4. _____ ○
5. _____ ○

SUNDAY LIST

1. _____ ○
2. _____ ○
3. _____ ○
4. _____ ○
5. _____ ○

DIGITAL DETOX ⬤   SELF-CARE SUNDAY ⬤   HAVE FUN ⬤

GOALS FOR NEXT WEEK

_____

_____

_____

_____

MIND DUMP

GRATITUDE LETTER

Take a moment to reflect on someone in your life you deeply appreciate, then write them a heartfelt letter expressing your gratitude. Cultivate a sense of connection and appreciation in your relationship.

Dear

_____

_____

_____

_____

_____

_____

_____

_____

_____

_____

_____

_____

_____

_____

_____

_____

_____

_____

EACH DAY IS AN OPPORTUNITY TO START AFRESH

SLEEP TRACKER MOOD TRACKER WATER TRACKER

5.00
5.30
6.00
6.30
7.00
7.30
8.00
8.30
9.00
9.30
10.00
10.30
11.00
11.30
12.00
12.30
13.00
13.30
14.00
13.30
15.00
15.30
16.00
16.30
17.00
17.30
18.00
18.30
19.00
19.30
20.00
20.30
21.00
21.30
22.00

POWER HOUR

50-10 METHOD

1. _____
2. _____
3. _____
4. _____
5. _____

NOTES

Scan to
meditate:

One moment I want to remember from today is . . .

Who is someone I am cheering for?

I have looked after myself today by . . .

REMINDER: I WILL NOT BE TOO HARD ON MYSELF

SLEEP TRACKER

☾ ☾ ☾ ☾ ☾ ☾ ☾ ☾

MOOD TRACKER

☺ ☺ ☺ ☺ ☺

WATER TRACKER

▯ ▯ ▯ ▯ ▯ ▯ ▯ ▯

5.00	
5.30	
6.00	
6.30	
7.00	
7.30	
8.00	
8.30	
9.00	
9.30	
10.00	
10.30	
11.00	
11.30	
12.00	
12.30	
13.00	
13.30	
14.00	
13.30	
15.00	
15.30	
16.00	
16.30	
17.00	
17.30	
18.00	
18.30	
19.00	
19.30	
20.00	
20.30	
21.00	
21.30	
22.00	

POWER HOUR

○ _____
○ _____
○ _____
○ _____
○ _____
○ _____
○ _____
○ _____
○ _____
○ _____
○ _____
○ _____

50-10 METHOD

1. _____ ○
2. _____ ○
3. _____ ○
4. _____ ○
5. _____ ○

NOTES

Scan to
meditate:

One moment I want to remember from today is . . .

What makes me feel at ease?

I have looked after myself today by . . .

REST IS A REQUIREMENT, NOT A REWARD

SLEEP TRACKER	MOOD TRACKER	WATER TRACKER
🌙🌙🌙🌙🌙🌙🌙🌙	☺☺☺☺☺	▯▯▯▯▯▯▯▯

	POWER HOUR
5.00	○ _____
5.30	○ _____
6.00	○ _____
6.30	○ _____
7.00	○ _____
7.30	○ _____
8.00	○ _____
8.30	○ _____
9.00	○ _____
9.30	○ _____
10.00	○ _____
10.30	○ _____
11.00	○ _____
11.30	
12.00	
12.30	
13.00	
13.30	
14.00	
13.30	
15.00	
15.30	
16.00	
16.30	
17.00	**50-10 METHOD**
17.30	
18.00	1. _____ ○
18.30	
19.00	2. _____ ○
19.30	3. _____ ○
20.00	
20.30	4. _____ ○
21.00	5. _____ ○
21.30	
22.00	

NOTES

Scan to meditate:

One moment I want to remember from today is . . .

What is my favourite priceless feeling?

I have looked after myself today by . . .

APPRECIATING THE NOW IS POWERFUL
FOR MY TOMORROW

SLEEP TRACKER	MOOD TRACKER	WATER TRACKER
🌙🌙🌙🌙🌙🌙🌙🌙	😊😊😊😊😊	▯▯▯▯▯▯▯▯

	POWER HOUR
5.00	
5.30	○
6.00	
6.30	○
7.00	
7.30	○
8.00	
8.30	○
9.00	
9.30	○
10.00	
10.30	○
11.00	
11.30	○
12.00	
12.30	○
13.00	
13.30	○
14.00	
13.30	○
15.00	○

5.00
5.30
6.00
6.30
7.00
7.30
8.00
8.30
9.00
9.30
10.00
10.30
11.00
11.30
12.00
12.30
13.00
13.30
14.00
13.30
15.00
15.30
16.00
16.30
17.00
17.30
18.00
18.30
19.00
19.30
20.00
20.30
21.00
21.30
22.00

50-10 METHOD

1. _____ ○
2. _____ ○
3. _____ ○
4. _____ ○
5. _____ ○

NOTES

Scan to meditate:

One moment I want to remember from today is . . .

Who do I trust the most and why?

I have looked after myself today by . . .

IF I UPGRADE MY BELIEFS, I WILL WATCH MY LIFE IMPROVE

SLEEP TRACKER   MOOD TRACKER   WATER TRACKER

5.00	POWER HOUR
5.30	○
6.00	○
6.30	○
7.00	○
7.30	○
8.00	○
8.30	○
9.00	○
9.30	○
10.00	○
10.30	○
11.00	○
11.30	○
12.00	
12.30	
13.00	
13.30	
14.00	
13.30	
15.00	
15.30	
16.00	
16.30	
17.00	50-10 METHOD
17.30	1. ○
18.00	2. ○
18.30	3. ○
19.00	4. ○
19.30	5. ○
20.00	
20.30	
21.00	
21.30	
22.00	

NOTES

Scan to
meditate:

One moment I want to remember from today is . . .

_____

_____

My greatest skill is . . .

_____

_____

I have looked after myself today by . . .

_____

_____

IT IS OK TO HAVE A DIFFERENT JOURNEY TO OTHERS

SATURDAY LIST

1. _____ ○
2. _____ ○
3. _____ ○
4. _____ ○
5. _____ ○

SUNDAY LIST

1. _____ ○
2. _____ ○
3. _____ ○
4. _____ ○
5. _____ ○

DIGITAL DETOX ⬤   SELF-CARE SUNDAY ⬤   HAVE FUN ⬤

GOALS FOR NEXT WEEK

_____
_____
_____
_____

MIND DUMP

WHAT MY FUTURE TELLS ME

 Put yourself ahead into the future. What do you see? Write it in the crystal ball below.

MY MONTHLY WORK–LIFE BALANCE WHEEL

 On a scale of 1 to 10, how am I feeling in the following areas of my work and life? Do not overthink it, just colour it in!

1 ————————————————————— **10**

NOT-SO-GREAT   GREAT

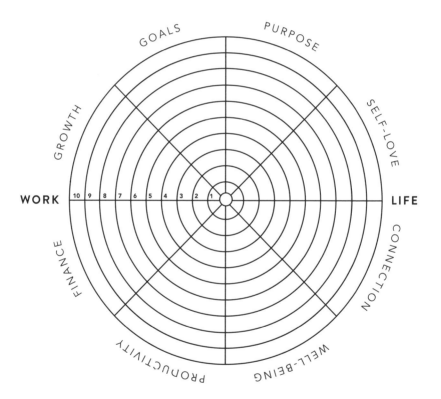

 Tip: Use the space around the wheel to note ways in which you can add more balance to your life.

MY MONTHLY REVIEW

WHAT WENT WELL THIS MONTH?

DID I STRUGGLE WITH ANYTHING THIS MONTH?

IS THERE ANYTHING I COULD HAVE DONE DIFFERENTLY?

WHAT THREE EMOTIONS RULED MY ENERGY THIS MONTH?

HOW CAN I ADD MORE BALANCE INTO MY LIFE GOING FORWARD?

WHAT IS ONE THING I WANT TO START/DO/ACHIEVE NEXT MONTH?

MY PROFESSIONAL REFLECTIONS

WHAT WAS MY HIGHLIGHT FROM THE LAST 6 MONTHS?

HOW DID I HANDLE ANY STRESSES?

HOW HAVE I PRIORITIZED MY WELL-BEING?

IS THERE ANYTHING I WANT TO DO MORE OR LESS OF?

WHAT IS NEXT FOR ME PROFESSIONALLY?

MY PERSONAL REFLECTIONS

WHAT WAS MY HIGHLIGHT FROM THE LAST 6 MONTHS?

HOW DID I HANDLE ANY STRESSES?

HOW HAVE I PRIORITIZED MY WELL-BEING?

IS THERE ANYTHING I WANT TO DO MORE OR LESS OF?

WHAT IS NEXT FOR ME PERSONALLY?

NOTES

NOTES

NOTES

NOTES

I PLANNED, I PERFORMED AND I AM PROUD OF THE PROGRESS I MADE ONE DAY AND ONE MOMENT AT A TIME.